Souvenir from TOLCHESTER BEACH, MD.

Washed Ashore.

BETTERTON, MD.

19672

TOLCHESTER

STEAMBOAT DAYS ON THE CHESAPEAKE

BETTERTON AND TOLCHESTER BEACH, MARYLAND

James A. Tigner, Jr.

Schiffer Publishing Ltd

4880 Lower Valley Road, Atglen, Pennsylvania 19310

ACKNOWLEDGMENTS

My sincerest thank you goes to William K. Betts, the Curator of the Tolchester Beach Revisited Museum. Bill graciously spent time with me discussing Tolchester Beach and offered words of enthusiasm for this project. He also graciously opened up his museum one winter morning especially for me and allowed me to photograph as I pleased. The museum, devoted to preserving the memory of Tolchester Beach, is located in Rock Hall, Maryland.

Other Schiffer Books by James Tigner, Jr.
Annapolis Reflections. ISBN: 978-0-7643-3157-2. $29.99
Chincoteague Island. ISBN: 9780764329197. $29.99
Colonial Beach, Virginia. ISBN: 9780764328084. $24.99
Greetings from Hampton Roads, Virginia. ISBN: 9780764328367. $34.99
Greetings from Virginia Beach. ISBN: 9780764329999. $29.99
Memories of Chesapeake Beach & North Beach, Maryland. ISBN: 9780764327681. $24.95
St. Michaels, Oxford, and the Talbot County Bayside. ISBN: 9780764327087. $39.95
Yesterday on the Chesapeake Bay. ISBN: 0764325973. $39.95

Other Schiffer Books on Related Subjects
Greetings from Annapolis. Mary Martin & Nathaniel Wolfgang-Price. ISBN: 0764326007. $19.95
The U. S. Naval Academy in Postcards. Randall W. Bannister. ISBN: 9780764331084. $39.99

Copyright © 2009 by James A. Tigner, Jr.
Library of Congress Control Number: 2009929805

Designed by Mark David Bowyer
Type set in EngraversRoman Bd BT / Humanist 521 BT

ISBN: 978-0-7643-3109-1
Printed in China

Schiffer Books are available at special discounts for bulk purchases for sales promotions or premiums. Special editions, including personalized covers, corporate imprints, and excerpts can be created in large quantities for special needs. For more information contact the publisher:

Published by Schiffer Publishing Ltd.
4880 Lower Valley Road
Atglen, PA 19310
Phone: (610) 593-1777; Fax: (610) 593-2002
E-mail: Info@schifferbooks.com

For the largest selection of fine reference books on this and related subjects,
please visit our web site at **www.schifferbooks.com**
We are always looking for people to write books on new and related subjects.
If you have an idea for a book please contact us at the above address.

This book may be purchased from the publisher.
Include $5.00 for shipping.
Please try your bookstore first.
You may write for a free catalog.

In Europe, Schiffer books are distributed by
Bushwood Books
6 Marksbury Ave.
Kew Gardens
Surrey TW9 4JF England
Phone: 44 (0) 20 8392 8585; Fax: 44 (0) 20 8392 9876
E-mail: info@bushwoodbooks.co.uk
Website: www.bushwoodbooks.co.uk

CONTENTS

Waiting for the Tide to come in.

Bathing Beach, Betterton, Md.

THE GOAT TRACK, TOLCHESTER BEACH, MD.

THE CHESAPEAKE, BETTERTON, MD.

INTRODUCTION

At one time the two most popular destinations for summertime fun and excitement on the Maryland portion of the Chesapeake Bay were Betterton and Tolchester Beach. Both owed their popularity to the steamboat. To be more precise, they both rode the wave of popularity created by the excursion steamer. Modern maps reveal Betterton and the site of Tolchester Beach to be far removed from the busy highway, and by today's way of thinking, they are out-of-the-way places. Tolchester Beach was located directly on the Chesapeake Bay in Kent County; Betterton, also in Kent County, is at the mouth of the Sassafras River. When the Chesapeake Bay and its rivers were nautical pathways just as important as today's modern highways, Betterton and Tolchester Beach were ideally situated. They could not have been more popular in their day, and everyone who wanted to go someplace for summertime fun went to either Betterton or Tolchester Beach.

With its beach and amusement area and many hotels, Betterton was the ideal place to spend an extended vacation. Betterton's hotels, however, were not like the hotels we know today. The hotels at Betterton looked more like large wooden houses and, in many ways, just a much enlarged version of one's own home. At these hotels, each with its big wrap-around porch and wooden glider swing in the front yard, families boarded, took their meals, had their laundry needs taken care of, and casually socialized and made friends with other families. Families vacationed at Betterton for several days, a week, two weeks; many families stayed the entire summer.

Although Tolchester Beach did have a hotel, the Hotel Tolchester, it was primarily a place where one went to in the morning and returned home from late in the evening. In other words, for the great majority of its visitors, Tolchester Beach was a day park. To be more precise, Tolchester Beach was an excursion boat ride, an amusement park, a bathing beach, and a picnic ground all rolled into one. As such, Tolchester Beach was the ideal destination for families. Often a family went to Tolchester Beach with other families and these groups of families would know and socialize with each other at the park. Whole boatloads of families arrived together at Tolchester Beach; the steamboat *Louise* would bring 2,500 passengers at a time. Families came to Tolchester Beach as part of church groups, employee groups, civic and business groups, as club, school, fraternal, and other similar groups. Each family brought a large picnic basket filled with home cooked food and every young person of school age and older had a pocket full of saved up coins to buy tickets for the rides. In the evening the picnic baskets went home empty, no one went home hungry, happy memories were many, and the coins left in a young person's pocket were few if any.

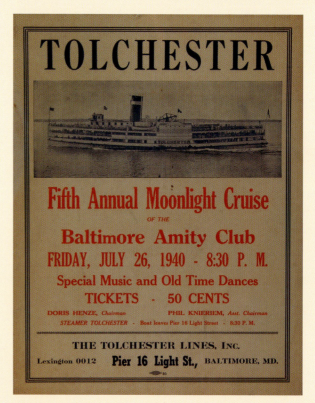

Advertising sign for the fifth annual moonlight cruise of the Baltimore Amity Club on Friday, July 26, 1940, aboard the steamer *Tolchester*. The steamer ferried excursionists between Baltimore and Tolchester Beach from 1933 until the end of the 1940 season. The *Tolchester* burned at her Light Street pier in May 1941. The cause of the fire was never determined.

The *Sarah K. Taggart* was the first steamboat to ply between Baltimore and Tolchester Beach.

Walkway at Tolchester Beach. Circa 1950s. *Courtesy of Tolchester Beach Revisited Museum.*

Souvenir pennant, *S. S. Bay Belle*, Wilson Line. Circa 1950s.

Police security badge, Wilson-Tolchester Steamship Company, *S. S. Bay Belle*. Circa 1958-60.

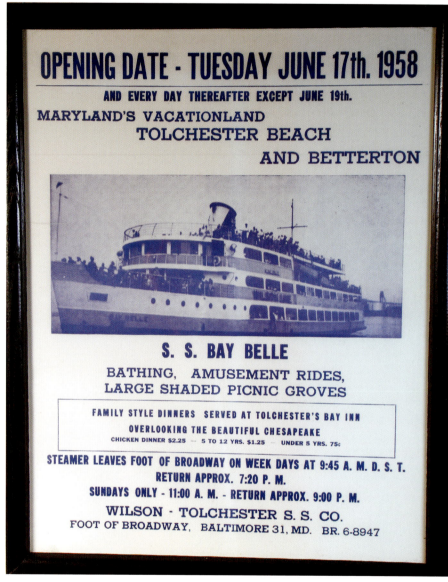

Poster advertising excursions to Betterton and Tolchester Beach. Circa 1958. *Courtesy of Tolchester Beach Revisited Museum.*

The History of Betterton

In 1850, Richard Thompson Turner, a successful Baltimore merchant, purchased 180 acres of land in the rural northern part of Kent County. The following year he packed up his possessions, said goodbye to Baltimore, and moved to his new property, which was a little over three miles north of the small town of Still Pond. Turner's family roots were firmly planted in the Eastern Shore and he no doubt felt that by moving to Kent County he was returning to where he belonged. On his property he built his home, which he called Ellwood, and with his wife Elizabeth, raised a large family. Turner was still a young man when he arrived in Kent County. Only in his thirties at the time, he busied himself with a number of different endeavors, primarily the overseeing of a sawmill he had established. Turner's property was about a half-mile from the Sassafras River. In 1855 he purchased several acres of land directly on the river below his house and erected a steamboat wharf, warehouse, granary, and a store. It was also at this location that he oversaw his lumber business.

Turner's waterfront enterprises were ideally situated. Here was an area where the upper waters of the Chesapeake Bay merged and mixed with those of the Susquehanna, Northeast, Elk, and Sassafras Rivers. His waterfront property was on the south side and at the mouth of the Sassafras River. The property faced due north and not too far distant were the waterfront towns of Havre de Grace and Perryville at the mouth of the Susquehanna River, Charlestown and North East on the Northeast River, and Elkton at the headwaters of the Elk River. Georgetown and Fredericktown were located farther up the Sassafras River from Turner's property. Via the steamboats and large sailing schooners that docked at his wharf, Turner shipped the lumber being turned out by his sawmill. Turner's wharf was also popular with farmers shipping produce, and an important landing for the coming and going of freight in general. In only a few years after his arrival, Turner was the area's largest employer and also its most influential citizen.

The area in which Turner had built his home and businesses had long been informally known as Crew's Landing. The "Crew" family name in the Betterton area can be traced back to Edward Crew, who leased land in 1715 and then purchased sixty acres of land in 1726. When Turner arrived in 1851, "Crew" was one of the dominant names in the area. However, no one seemed to object when Turner bestowed the area with the name Betterton. In choosing the name Betterton, he honored his wife, for that was her maiden name. For the most part, the land area that made up Crew's Landing, and what we know today as Betterton, was originally a land grant from Lord Baltimore to William Fisher for 225 acres. The land granted to Fisher in 1664 was called "Fishall." In time the area took on the name "Fish Hall." As with many early names, the reason for the name "Fishall" or "Fish Hall" is uncertain and lost to the passage of time. It is possible that the name Fish Hall is a corruption of "Fish Haul;" for commercial fishing had been actively pursued throughout the area since colonial times. Furthermore, a small fishing village of some degree existed in the area years before the name "Crew's Landing" or "Betterton" was used. H. Chandlee Forman, in his book *The Rolling Year on Maryland's Upper Eastern Shore*, makes a good point when he comments: *The name could have been a pun on 'Fisher,' i.e., 'Fisher's-all' or 'Fish-all.'* At any rate, as already discussed, over time the area became informally known as Crew's Landing, and then, after Turner arrived, was renamed Betterton.

Betterton's transformation into a beach resort began in the 1860s when the Chesapeake House, a two and one-half story hotel, was built. In the 1880s Turner built an "Amusement Pier." Not too much is known about its early use, but by 1900 the Amusement Pier was a two story structure offering dancing, bowling, boating, and fishing. Around the same time Turner's Amusement Pier was constructed, the Baltimore and Philadelphia Steamboat Company (Ericsson Line) built a substantial 700 foot pier at the west end of the beach. Their boats brought excursionists from Baltimore, Philadelphia, Chester, and Wilmington to Betterton. By the end of the 1890s, Betterton had become a popular and well-known beach resort destination. While visitors to beaches further down the Chesapeake Bay had to put up with the nuisance and stings of sea nettles, Betterton's beach was nettle free. This was due to the low salt content of the water in the upper Chesapeake. In 1899 the Tolchester Beach Improvement

Company purchased the "Betterton Wharf" and it also became known as the "Tolchester Pier." Two of the company's boats, the *Susquehanna* and the *Sassafras* (later renamed *Annapolis*), began calling regularly at the resort.

An Ericsson Line promotional brochure for the year 1915 is informative. During the summer months their vessels departed Baltimore and Philadelphia daily at 8 a.m. This meant an arrival time at Betterton for the boat from Baltimore of around 11 a.m. and around 5 p.m. for the boat from Philadelphia. The one-way fare between Baltimore and Betterton was forty cents. From Philadelphia the one-way fare was one dollar. The Ericsson Line fleet of vessels at the time included the *Anthony Groves, Jr.* built in 1893, the *Ericsson* built in 1897, and the sister ships *Penn* and *Lord Baltimore*, both built in 1902. The Ericsson Line boats were different from others in one distinct way; they had all been built to specifications that allowed them to traverse the Chesapeake & Delaware Canal. Before the canal was greatly improved in 1927, it was a narrow causeway with a number of locks. The large Ericsson Line boats had to have very narrow beams to be able to fit in the locks and to pass other vessels in the canal. For this reason it was easy to tell an Ericsson Line boat from one of another line, especially when viewed head on or from directly astern. The early boats of the Baltimore and Philadelphia Steamboat Company were also some of the first to be driven by a propeller instead of big side-wheels. The ship propeller was invented by John Ericsson in 1833, hence the origin of the use of the more informal name – Ericsson Line.

During its heyday, 1900 until the mid-1950s, Betterton averaged around twenty different places to stay at any one time. Permanent, year round residents living at Betterton averaged three hundred, but on a typical summer weekend the population could swell to upwards of three to four thousand individuals. Betterton's hotels were for the most part large and rambling, multi-storied Victorian wooden structures. The typical hotel had a large wrap around porch with a long row of wooden rockers, from which guests relaxed and looked out onto a manicured, fenced, and tree shaded yard. Full course country meals, served family style, were usually included in the rent. Almost always the fish had been caught locally that morning and oftentimes the tomatoes and other vegetables had just been picked hours earlier at one of the outlying local farms or even grown in the backyard garden of the hotel. Since families tended to return year after year to the same establishment, the proprietor was often considered a friend and known on a first name basis. The slowed down country atmosphere at these establishments created many opportunities for different families to become acquainted with each other. Sometimes even a new summertime romance was sparked under a full moon and in an arbor shielding, quiet corner of a hotel's manicured lawn. More than once a husband and wife could nostalgically boast that they had first met years ago as teenagers while their respective families vacationed for a week or two at a Betterton hotel.

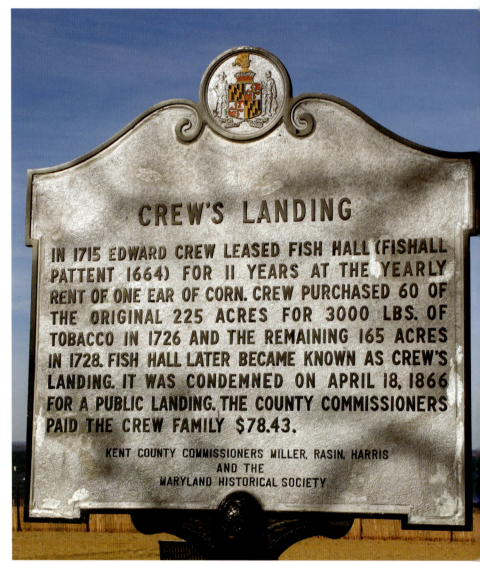

CREW'S LANDING

IN 1715 EDWARD CREW LEASED FISH HALL (FISHALL PATTENT 1664) FOR 11 YEARS AT THE YEARLY RENT OF ONE EAR OF CORN. CREW PURCHASED 60 OF THE ORIGINAL 225 ACRES FOR 3000 LBS. OF TOBACCO IN 1726 AND THE REMAINING 165 ACRES IN 1728. FISH HALL LATER BECAME KNOWN AS CREW'S LANDING. IT WAS CONDEMNED ON APRIL 18, 1866 FOR A PUBLIC LANDING. THE COUNTY COMMISSIONERS PAID THE CREW FAMILY $78.43.

KENT COUNTY COMMISSIONERS MILLER, RASIN, HARRIS
AND THE
MARYLAND HISTORICAL SOCIETY

Historical marker at Betterton.

As reported by the Betterton Chamber of Commerce, the following hotels, inns, and cottages were available for vacationers in 1952: "Betterton Hotel, Chesapeake Hotel, Country Cousin Inn, The Ferncliffe, The Fleetwood, The Maplewood Inn, Rigbie Hotel, Sykes Cottage, The Atlantic, The Betterview, Bower's Cottage, Buena Vista, The Four Gables, Harhan Hill, The Idlewhile, Jewell Cottage, The Chesapeake Cottages, Evergreen Knoll, Rodman's Cottages, and the Lewis' Apartments." Of all of these establishments, the Chesapeake Hotel (originally the Chesapeake House) was the oldest, the biggest, and the most popular. The hotel could not be missed, as it was located right next to the sandy beach. Over the years the hotel was enlarged and improved several times, until rising to five stories. The Chesapeake Hotel closed for good in 1973 and was razed in 1980. The Rigbie Hotel, another well-known establishment, was erected in 1902. The Rigbie Hotel could accommodate upwards of 150 to 175 guests at any one time. Per a brochure published by the Country Cousin Inn in the mid-1950s, a weeklong stay for two (including two meals a day) at that inn cost sixty dollars a week. The brochure goes on to say: "*At this cozy cottage, we offer a site that is close to the beach, where bathing is allowed from the house. Our meals served country style, are fine, offering on their menus breads and pastries made at our own Inn.*"

A familiar site at Betterton throughout the summer months during the last half of the 1940s and continuing through the 1950s was the coming and going of the *Bay Belle*. The Wilson Line began operating the excursion boat between Baltimore and Betterton in June 1946. The two hundred foot *Bay Belle* could carry 2,400 passengers on her spacious four decks. A 1951 Wilson Line promotional brochure described the *Bay Belle* as the: "*Pride of the Chesapeake.*" The boat would leave Baltimore from the Excursion Pier at the foot of Broadway at 9:45 a.m., cruise to Betterton, lay over for a few hours, and then head back, arriving in Baltimore at 7:15 p.m. After a one-hour layover in Baltimore, just long enough to discharge passengers and pick up a new load of passengers, the boat would depart for a three hour moonlight dance cruise. The same 1951 Wilson Line brochure states: "*The Bay Belle takes a cool, northerly route to Betterton by day, and sails as a dance cruiser every evening.*" Every Sunday evening in 1951 WBAL-TV televised a popular half-hour dance show called "Aboard the *Bay Belle*." Excursions to Betterton aboard the *Bay Belle* ended in 1962. The last excursion boat to cruise between Baltimore and Betterton was the *MV Port Welcome*. The boat made the trip several times a week during the summer months throughout the 1960s and 1970s.

Today Betterton survives, yet in a relaxed and retiring residential slumber. The town's year round population has remained about the same since its resort days. Betterton's water views are enduring and some of the finest in the entire upper Chesapeake Bay region. Although the beach is still available and is now a public park, the piers, the steamboats, the amusements, the dance hall, and the bathhouse, as well as streets full of cars constantly arriving and departing are all gone. Betterton's two largest and most popular hotels during its halcyon resort days, the Rigbie and the Chesapeake, are gone too. Other old hotels from the resort era still stand, yet as private residences. Mixed in with the old are new townhouses and condos. The feeling one gets these days while walking around Betterton is that the town is being silently reminiscent and reverent in regard to its past; nostalgia seems to float wistfully everywhere in the air.

Welcome sign at Betterton.

THE HISTORY OF TOLCHESTER BEACH

Seeing what looked like a golden opportunity to capitalize on the new demand for steamboat service, which would arise when a railway line being built across Kent County, Maryland, to the shores of the Chesapeake Bay was completed, a father and son team of steamboat operators on the Delaware River and Bay joined forces with a steamboat operator on the Potomac River. The year was 1876 and the tracks of the Kent County Railroad had already been laid some twenty miles in a hook-like fashion from the Maryland / Delaware line through Massys, Lambsons, Kennedyville, Still Pond, Worton, and continued on to Chestertown. Now work was progressing on building the road-bed and laying track to a place that the railroad called Nicholson Station, about four miles southwest from Worton. Plans called for the railroad to rendezvous with steamboats on the Chesapeake Bay at two locations. One location was to be the rural area known as Tolchester. The other location was Deep Landing (Rock Hall), which was a bustling fishing village five miles farther south.

The golden opportunity that presented itself to Calvin Taggart, his son E. B. Taggart, and John Ambruster was the "for sale" sign recently hung on the one thousand plus acres known as the Tolchester Farm. The Tolchester Farm fronted on the Chesapeake Bay and included the proposed and coveted site for the Tolchester terminal. The exact agreement that the three steamboat men entered into is unknown but the two Taggarts from Philadelphia and Ambruster who hailed from nearby Camden, New Jersey, shook hands and moved quickly. John Ambruster purchased the farm during the summer of 1876 and contracted to have a steamboat pier constructed soon thereafter.

While the three steamboat men were moving forward with their plans, all was not going well financially with the railroad. Over the winter the Kent County Railroad went bankrupt. Then on February 15, 1877, ownership of the railroad changed hands in a foreclosure sale. This must have been disturbing and disappointing news for the steamboat men but they continued with their plans and later that month the Taggarts brought over one of their boats to initiate steamboat service between Baltimore and Tolchester. The *Sarah K. Taggart* had been built in 1875 and was 155 feet in length. During the summer of 1877 the

Sarah K. Taggart hauled freight when it could get the business and periodically brought small excursion groups from Baltimore to Tolchester. The Baltimoreans who took the steamboat to Tolchester that summer stretched their legs along the shoreline, waded in the surf, picnicked, joked, and laughed; some just sat quietly among the shade trees and soaked up the country air for a few hours before the boat took them back to the city. Sometime during the spring or summer of 1877, and surely with the intent to give more of a recreational sound to the name, Tolchester was renamed Tolchester Beach. Meanwhile, the laying of track for the railroad was advancing at a very slow rate. By the end of 1877, rails had been laid only to a place the railroad called Parsons, which was about eight miles beyond Worton. The following year saw even less progress being made by the railroad and its roadbed was still a number of miles from both Tolchester and Deep Landing. In the end, the railroad never reached either location. The original vision of the steamboat men to make Tolchester a hub of railroad activity connecting with steamboats arriving from up and down the Chesapeake Bay was not to be.

Views of Tolchester Beach in the 1950s.

The year was 1878 and with all hope for the railroad to reach Tolchester dashed, the two Taggarts and Ambruster took a closer look at their Tolchester Beach property. The question for them was – to sell the property, almost certainly at a loss, and move on or keep the property and try to make a go of things without the business that the railroad would have brought. The property's natural attributes were a sandy beach, plenty of shade trees, and from the top of the bluff there was a commanding panoramic view of the beautiful Chesapeake Bay below. However, the property was far out in the rural Kent County countryside; still though, in relation to Baltimore, only twenty-six water miles by steamboat, it was ideally situated. Then there was the brand new steamboat pier to consider. The consensus of the steamboat men was unanimous – build a resort catering to the recreational desires of Baltimoreans.

For reasons not known today, other than that her owners deemed her "unsatisfactory," the *Sarah K. Taggart* was withdrawn. In 1878, the steamer *Pilot Boy* began operating on the route. Built in 1857 at Wilmington, Delaware, *Pilot Boy* was 161 feet in length and had a beam of twenty-two and a half feet. At this same time an enterprising and enthusiastic employee, William C. Eliason, who had already proved his worth and been promoted several times by the Taggarts, was given the opportunity to buy into the resort idea by purchasing a one-fourth share of the ownership of *Pilot Boy*. An added bonus for Eliason's earnest money was that he was promoted again. This time the Taggarts made him general manager, overseeing all excursion and freight business between Baltimore and Tolchester Beach under their newly formed corporation, the Tolchester Steamboat Company.

Eliason immersed himself in his new role with all the zest and zeal that had earned him the position to begin with. His first order of business had been to head for Baltimore and locate suitable dock, freight, and office space for the new steamboat company. He arranged for the company to rent Pier 9 ½ on Baltimore's Light Street. During the temperate days of April and May, Eliason stayed busy drumming up excursion business for the month of June and what he hoped would be many hot, dry, and steamy days in July and August. With air conditioning still years away, the only relief many city dwellers had from the summer's sweltering heat was a splash on the face with water hand pumped from a well, or an evening, sometimes an entire night, spent under a tree in one of the city's parks. Elisaon knew many Baltimoreans would be enticed to take the trip to Tolchester if only to relish in a few hours of Bay breezes, even if they were manufactured artificially by the ship making headway, and to have the opportunity to frolic, wade, and swim in the cool waters of the Chesapeake

Ticket, excursion to Tolchester Beach aboard the *Sarah K. Taggart*, Monday, July 9th, 1877, leaving Pier 11, Light Street at 8 a.m. Actual size 2" x 4" Note: The author considers this well worn ticket to be the scarcest piece of Tolchester Beach ephemera that he has seen. It was found by the author amongst a pile of miscellaneous papers at a Baltimore flea market.

The steamer *Pilot Boy* was the second steamboat to ply between Baltimore and Tolchester Beach. *Courtesy of Tolchester Beach Revisited Museum.*

Bay. From the start the excursions to Tolchester Beach were promoted as being alcohol free. Both on the boat and at the park, no liquor was sold, nor could any be consumed. The company's temperance stand was a negative to some and an inducement to others. The decision not to allow alcohol was probably made as much for business reasons as it was for moral or religious reasons. By banning alcoholic beverages, the company would certainly have less of a problem with rowdy or out of control individuals. The excursions to Tolchester Beach would also appeal more to families, church groups, and business organizations.

Baltimoreans embraced the new excursions to Tolchester Beach with great enthusiasm. All summer long *Pilot Boy*, loaded to capacity with six hundred happy excursionists, steamed out of Baltimore's harbor, headed towards the mouth of the Patapsco River, and then up and across the Chesapeake Bay to Tolchester Beach. Pleased greatly with the patronage of their new excursion boat business, the company continued to improve the Tolchester Beach property. The Tolchester pier was made larger, picnic tables were multiplied, and a new bathhouse, a hotel, and concessions were added to the park grounds.

With the exuberant and focused energy of Eliason, the Tolchester Beach excursion continued to be well patronized and grew in popularity with each summer season. In 1881, *Pilot Boy* was deemed to be too small and the company began looking for a larger boat. The company purchased the *Nelly White* from a New York concern. Launched in 1866, the *Nelly White* was 181 feet in length and had a beam of twenty-nine feet. *Nelly White* could carry 900 passengers. In 1882 the company found a buyer for the unused acreage that had been a part of its original Tolchester land purchase. By selling all but the thirty acres being used for the park, the company was able to pay for many of the improvements it was making to the park at the time. Also in 1882, the steamer *Louise* was purchased by the company. The *Louise* had been built in 1864 and had a length of 232 feet and a beam of thirty-three feet. *Louise* was the largest steamboat the company had owned so far. Baltimoreans were quick to embrace and fall in love with the *Louise*. The steamboat rarely left Baltimore with fewer than the 2,500 passengers her three decks could hold.

Since the debut of the steamboat *Louise* on the Baltimore to Tolchester Beach route, the *Nelly White* had been seen rarely at the Tolchester pier. However she still served an important role for the company. Over the last several years the company had broadened its sights beyond running excursions to just Tolchester Beach. Several subsidiary steamboat companies had been formed with routes to various landings and wharfs on a number of different rivers on the Chesapeake. One of the routes was from Baltimore to St. Michaels and other landings on the Miles River in Talbot County.

In August of 1886 the *Nelly White* was involved in a collision with a sailing vessel near Sandy Point. The *Nelly White* sank in shallow water. Damage to the vessel was extensive and did not warrant repairs. However the boiler and engine were salvaged from the wreck. The company immediately sought a replacement for the *Nelly White*. This time however, the company decided to have a new steamboat built.

Just six months after the unfortunate *Nelly White* mishap, the company had its new steamboat. On March 2, 1887, a five-year-old girl was given the honor of christening the *Emma Giles*, which had been named after her. Her father was a successful Baltimore businessman at the time and he had extended to the Tolchester Steamboat Company most of the money needed to have the vessel built. When the *Emma Giles* made her trial run to Tolchester Beach in June she was the pride and joy of the company. The *Emma Giles* had a length of 178 feet and a beam of thirty and a-half feet. Designed to carry both passengers and freight, she had space for around 1,000 passengers. Many years later in a *Baltimore Sun* "I Remember When" newspaper article dated September 25, 1949, Emma Giles Parker recalled the day she christened the boat: "*My father steadied my hand, and at a signal around noon, in my loudest voice I said: In the name of the Tolchester Steamboat Company, I name thee Emma Giles.*" When as a new vessel, the *Emma Giles* slid down the ways at the Woodall Shipyard where she had been built into the waters of a branch of the Patapsco River, she was not however 100 percent completely new. Her boiler and engine, which by the way served her well for all of her days, were the ones that had been salvaged from the old *Nelly White*.

In 1887 a subsidiary of the Tolchester Steamboat Company was formed. This was the Tolchester Beach Improvement Company. The purpose of the new company was to further the improvements and expansion of the Tolchester Beach property. Excursions to Tolchester Beach continued to be well patronized and an excellent moneymaker throughout the 1890s. Piers 16 and 17 on Light Street were purchased in 1898. In 1899 the original Tolchester Steamboat Company and its three subsidiary companies were combined into just one company. As such the Tolchester Steamboat Company, the Chesapeake Steamboat Company and the Port Deposit and Havre de Grace Steamboat Company all came under the control of the Tolchester Beach Improvement Company.

It was the best of times to be in the excursion boat and pleasure park business and the Tolchester Beach Improvement Company was prospering. The *Louise* was always loaded to capacity and the park at Tolchester bustled with excursionists. Over time the company was able to purchase back parcels of land it had originally sold off, and the park eventually grew in size to over 150 acres. An announcement appeared in the *Baltimore American* newspaper on June 30, 1889, titled "Tolchester's New Dress" and it read as follows: "*She is ready for excursionist now. Yesterday was inspection day at Tolchester Beach and a good crowd was taken down on both trips of the Louise. The improvements are many, and the visitors were surprised and delighted at the changes. The bathing-house at the beach has been moved up to a more desirable location. The approach from the long* pier looks inviting and the beach has been cleared so that pleasant walks may be taken. Along the beach are large shade trees, and flowerbeds are placed along the walks. There is a new switch-back railroad and a dairy lunch room, which adjoins the large dancing pavilion. Twenty-five acres of land have been added to the resort, and it has all been improved. There is a riding track and a racetrack, and the latter has a grand stand, where visitors may see the races. It has a seating capacity of one thousand and in the open field in front of the stands is plenty of space for out-door sports. There is a half-mile track, and just inside of it is a one-quarter of a mile track. Manager Wm. C. Eliason has provided attractions that are sure to please his patrons and they will be introduced from time to time during the season. There is a good restaurant, where a first-class meal may be had for fifty cents. The steamer Louise will make two trips daily during the season."

Circa 1890s-1910 photograph. *Courtesy of Tolchester Beach Revisited Museum.*

Tolchester Steamboat Company Pier 16 on Light Street, Baltimore. *Courtesy of Tolchester Beach Revisited Museum.*

Shortly after 8 p.m. on Monday, July 28, 1890, the steamer *Louise* collided with the *Virginia* of the Old Bay Line. The *Louise* was returning from Tolchester Beach with about 1,500 excursionists onboard when the incident occurred near Fort Carroll on the Patapsco River. Fifteen of the *Louise's* passengers lost their lives, three were killed instantly, ten drowned, and two died later from their injuries. A number of other passengers onboard the *Louise*, including several rescued from the water, were also injured. There were no deaths or injuries onboard the *Virginia*. The *Louise* had been badly damaged on her starboard side but she managed, after first stopping at Henderson's Wharf, to reach Light Street without needing assistance. One father had come down to the Light Street pier to meet his family. He soon learned that the *Louise* had been involved in an accident. As soon as the *Louise* pulled up to the pier he jumped onboard and searched the boat but was unable to find any members of his family among the living or the dead. His heart sank as he concluded that all of them had been drowned. Grief turned to euphoric joy when he was told that his family members had exited the boat at Henderson's Wharf. Although tragic, this was the only serious accident in which the *Louise* was involved during her forty-three years of service as an excursion boat crossing the Chesapeake Bay between Baltimore and Tolchester.

At the end of the 1897 season, the company reported that it had been their best season in twenty years of operation. During the regular season, which went from the middle of June until the middle of September, a newspaper article dated September 18, 1897, reported that, *"upwards of 400,000 persons had been carried to Tolchester."* If one interprets that figure to be a tally of only those arriving by boat, one can only guess how many more arrived by horse and buggy from Chestertown and other places in Kent County and beyond. The popularity of the Tolchester Beach excursion during the boom times of the 1890s and the remarkable success of the *Emma Giles* since it had been launched as a new boat were reason enough for the company to embark on building another steamboat. In 1898 the company christened the *Susquehanna* as its new steamer.

The *Susquehanna* was built by Charles Reeder & Sons at Baltimore, Maryland. The boat had a length of 158 feet, a beam of thirty-eight feet, and it was propeller driven as opposed to having side-wheels. The new vessel was put under the control of the Port Deposit and Havre de Grace Steamboat Company, a subsidiary of the Tolchester Steamboat Company. As mentioned earlier, these two companies were consolidated into the Tolchester Beach Improvement Company in 1899. The *Susquehanna* had been appropriately named as the company put her to work servicing the upper Chesapeake Bay landings, which included Havre de Grace, Perryville, and Port Deposit. The vessel could carry one thousand passengers. The *Susquehanna* had also been built to carry bulk cargo and freight, which included everything imaginable from farm produce and livestock, to furniture and store staples.

The assets of the Sassafras River Steamboat Company were purchased by the Tolchester Beach Improvement Company in 1899. Along with the purchase came two steamboats, the *Sassafras* and the *Van Corlaer the Trumpeter*. The latter was promptly renamed *Kitty Knight*. Most useful to the company was the larger *Sassafras*. Built in 1892, the *Sassafras* was 151 feet in length and had a beam of twenty-eight feet. *Sassafras* was placed on the Sassafras River route, which included the landings at Shallcross Wharf, Wilson Point Wharf, Cassidy Wharf, Georgetown, Fredericktown, and the popular summer resort known as Betterton. *Sassafras* was also used as a relief boat for the *Emma Giles* on its Annapolis and West River run. As with the *Emma Giles*, during the excursion season, *Sassafras* was used as an overflow boat picking up passengers still standing on the Tolchester pier after the steamer *Louise*, loaded to capacity, had departed on her return trip to Baltimore. In 1902 *Sassafras* was sent to the shipyard, emerged twenty-five feet longer, and was christened with a new name, the *Annapolis*. By 1924 much had changed. The company sent the steamer to the shipyard once more for modifications so that it could carry several automobiles in the bow area of its main deck. This was a modification that the vessel's builders could never have envisioned and a modification that certainly did nothing to improve the vessel's appearance. *Annapolis* burned at a company pier on Light Street in 1935. She was not burned beyond repair and had the company been in a stronger financial condition at the time, she probably would have been rebuilt. Instead *Annapolis* was abandoned and scratched from the company's list of assets.

Looking toward shore from the end of the excursion pier one would see the large entrance arch with the words "Tolchester Beach" emblazoned across it in Victorian lettering style and in big billboard size. Just to the left of the arch was the Excursion Pavilion, which had been built in 1909. The two-storied structure with its two towers was said to resemble an Italian renaissance villa. Rising still higher from each tower was an American flag. The pavilion had two levels. Its top level was used for dances, meetings, banquets, and similar functions. The first floor was nicknamed the "lower dairy" because of the huge amounts of ice cream and milk shakes that were sold there on any given summer day. The pavilion's large towers were generally the first images of Tolchester to appear on the horizon as the steamboat steamed towards the resort. Upon seeing the two towers from the hurricane (top) deck of the steamboat, children often pointed their fingers eastward, jumped up and down, and shouted words of excitement to their parents.

Further to the left and up on the hill from the Excursion Building was the Hotel Tolchester. The Hotel Tolchester had been built in the 1880s. The hotel was a four-story wooden structure with a panoramic view of the steamboat pier and the Chesapeake Bay. A company brochure widely distributed in the spring of 1935 describes the Hotel Tolchester as follows: *"This popular and well known hotel with hot and cold running water in rooms, large bright dining room, situated on* a high bluff overlooking the waters of the Chesapeake Bay, opens for the season June 10th. Surrounded as it is by well-shaded lawns, it offers many advantages over more famous resorts. The rooms are large and cheerful and overlook the bay or park as desired. Being in the midst of a farming community, we have unexcelled advantages for supplying the table with the best in the market. Then too, the fish and crabs taken out of the bay, insures them fresh and delicious at all times, making the table strictly first class. Adjoining the hotel are the famous Tolchester family excursion grounds, with acres of shady parks and amusements of every kind, where hundreds of excursionist are landed every day, from all over Maryland and adjacent states; the guests at the hotel are at liberty to ramble through the grounds, or select more quiet nooks just as they prefer. The mornings and evenings at Tolchester are usually cool and charming during most of the summer, and no one who has not visited the locality at that season can form any idea of how enjoyable the climate really is. A more delightful place to spend a few weeks during the summer would be hard to find." In 1935 a one-week stay at the hotel for two with running water cost thirty-two dollars per week. Without running water in the room, the cost was thirty dollars per week. A weekend stay at the hotel, which included supper on Saturday, and a send-off breakfast on Monday morning cost six dollars and fifty cents per individual. By 1948 rates had nearly doubled, as a weeklong stay at the hotel for two in a "bay view room with running water" cost sixty dollars. For the budget minded, a room overlooking the park grounds could be had for ten dollars less per week.

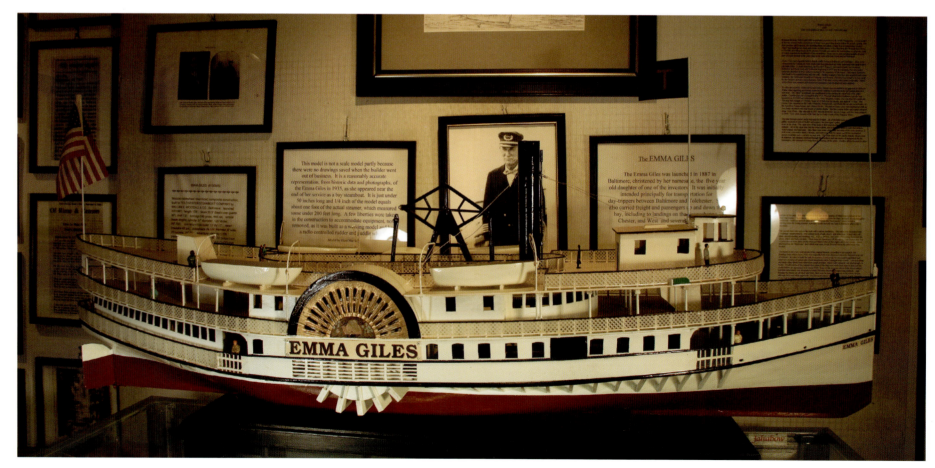

Model of the steamer *Emma Giles. Courtesy of Tolchester Beach Revisited Museum.*

In the picnic area families enjoyed their lunch while gathered around long weather worn tables, their tops decorated and draped with cloths in a multitude of patterns and in various colors. In between the shooing of flies, sometimes also yellow jacket bees, families feasted from large wooden baskets overflowing with fried chicken, hard boiled eggs, deviled eggs, and favorites like jelly sandwiches, ham and cheese sandwiches, and roast beef sandwiches. Biscuits, pickles, ripe tomato slices, scoops of coleslaw and potato salad, and a slice from a homemade pie or a layered cake complemented the main meal. All the while, these families consumed huge amounts of freshly squeezed, homemade lemonade. The entire meal was ever so slightly sprinkled with the coal dust and smoke that belched from the miniature railroad engine making its rounds and seasoned with the wind swept aroma of freshly steamed crabs and cooked fish escaping from the open windows of the hotel dining room.

There were only so many tables available in the picnic area. The lucky families getting a choice table, one with a view or in the shade of a tree, had to have a child who was fast on his or her feet. On any hot summer day, as the steamer pulled up alongside the pier, a designated child from each family group sprinted as fast as he or she could go down the length of the pier, through the entrance arch, up the steep hill, and into the picnic area. The child would make a selection and guard the table for his family by sitting squarely on its top. Then, ten or fifteen minutes later, the others lazily walked into the picnic area. Their picnic table, the base and center of the family activities for the day, was identified when mom and dad spotted their all smiling and proud child. Then there was always the child with gumption who used his running ability for his own benefit. After securing a choice table he would, just as quickly as he ran, sell the rights to use it to the first willing family.

In the heart of the park was the amusement area. Here were found assorted rides, games of chance, and concessions, which in one way or the other thrilled, challenged, or amused. In addition to motion pictures, entertainment for adults included the bingo parlor, the shooting gallery, and the bowling alley. Older children and teenagers had fun banging into each other with the bumper cars, as well as exploring the penny arcade and riding the Whip and the Whirlpool Dips roller coaster. For young children there were pony rides and a merry-go-round, as well as carts pulled by goats in which they could sit and race each other. Every one of all ages found great amusement in riding the miniature train, the boat rides on the lake, and the quaint "Tunnel of Love" ride. Cement, wood, and well-worn dirt pathways facilitated movement between the attractions, while several elevated walkways helped to smooth out the uneven terrain. To give a sense of unity to the park, many of its buildings had matching roofs and awnings in an alternating green and red striped pattern.

The souvenir stand sold everything from pennants to postcards. Any item that eluded one as a prize in the bingo parlor or at the games of chance booths could be purchased at the souvenir stand. Popular with the ladies were "ruby red flash glass," "custard glass," and green "Colorado glass." These souvenir glass items came in the shape of creamers, mugs, toothpick holders, tumblers, candy dishes, etc. Common to each piece of souvenir glass and printed in a prominent location was the wording, "Souvenir of Tolchester Park." Red roses stenciled all the way around or next to the lettering helped to decorate the pieces.

A popular item for a child was the souvenir pennant. Pennants were made of felt and came in various sizes and colors. All of the pennants said "Tolchester Beach" and along with tassels, most of them included a silk-screened image of a pretty beach girl as part of the decoration.

Tickets for the amusement park rides at Tolchester Beach.

Postcards, a very popular item with adults, ran the gauntlet of topics and themes but the biggest sellers were scenes of the park, picnic grounds, hotel, and pier. There was also the option to have a personalized photo postcard done in the Chenoweth Studio. Those being photographed tried not to move as the photographer took their picture against a draped generic and artificial seaside, rolling surf background. The souvenir glass items made the journey home carefully wrapped in a beach towel or hanky and packed in the bottom of picnic baskets. The postcards could be mailed at the park's own official United States post office, operational from 1879 until 1942. All of the mail, by the way, was individually hand-stamped. Unlike the souvenir glass and the postcards, many a child's big souvenir pennant never completed the journey home, for on the return boat ride and in a rush of air they were easily blown out of a child's hand, swept off the side of the boat, and swallowed up in the boats wake.

Looking toward shore, to the right of the entrance to the steamboat pier was the beach and bathing area. The bathhouse had bathing suits for rent and lockers to secure one's dry attire. Rowboats could be rented for fishing. Many young children from Baltimore, Chestertown, and the Kent County countryside took their first steps into the briny Chesapeake during the years when Tolchester was an active resort. Perhaps more than once the big event happened something like this – Mom would guide her young child, though just barely old enough to walk, down to the water's edge by holding both of his hands above his head. Afraid at seeing his first wave, the youngster stepped back and cried. Then, being naturally curious, he suddenly jumped forward to try and step on a wave and in doing so mom lost her grip on the youngster. Mom reached to pull him back. But at the same instant another wave washed around the youngster's feet. Loosing his balance, down on his knees he went and waves swirled around him. He giggled as mom pulled him to his feet. Then mom sat down in the wet sand and held her youngster firmly by the waist. After about two or three minutes of splashing in the waves, carrying on, and laughing, mom said something to the effect of "that is enough for now," and back up to the dry sand area they went. Dad, grandma, and the rest of the family had observed it all with great amusement. Then grandma would take the youngster from her daughter's arms and remind her daughter that it had been on the same beach that grandma had taken her and her brother for their first steps in the Chesapeake. When Grandma was asked by her daughter, grandma replied that she did not remember, but in all likelihood it was also at Tolchester Beach where grandma had taken her first steps into the briny Chesapeake Bay also.

Souvenir glass items from Tolchester Beach. Circa 1900-10.

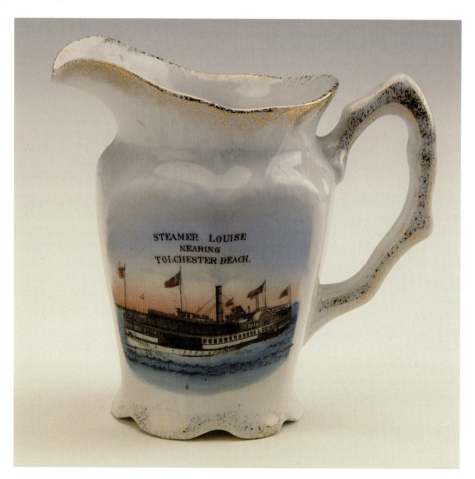

Souvenir creamer showing the "Steamer *Louise* nearing Tolchester Beach." Circa 1895-1905.

Everyone it seems loves a railroad. A miniature railroad, however, is looked upon with a special fondness. Such it was with the miniature railroad that was installed at Tolchester Beach in 1906. The little coal fired, steam driven train engine was called *Little Jumbo*. The engine pulled twelve brightly painted passenger cars, each of which had two seats facing one another. The miniature steam engine, modeled in many ways after a full size engine, was built in Baltimore by the Baldwin Locomotive Works. Perhaps as many adults rode the train as did children. A familiar sound at the park was *Little Jumbo's* whistle as it chugged across an open field, through the picnic grounds, around trees, over a bridge, and in and out of a tunnel. The train chugged along at a comfortable eight miles per hour, following its one quarter of a mile route. In the park's later days, it cost fifteen cents to ride the little train. Occasionally the engineer helped out a mom by warming her baby's bottle of formula on the engine's boiler. After the park closed, the miniature train went up to White Crystal Beach in nearby Cecil County. From there it went south to Harpers Ferry, West Virginia, and then north to Lancaster, Pennsylvania. Its whereabouts today are unknown.

January 16, 1920, was the day that marked the beginning of prohibition. However the 18th amendment had no effect on the policies of the Tolchester Company, for the company had never allowed alcoholic beverages on its boats or at its park. The 1920s were a time of many other changes though. With the 1920s came the flapper girl, the Bob cut, art deco, and a dance called the Charleston. The 1920s were also a time of change and new direction for the Tolchester Beach Improvement Company. William Eliason, who had been the company's driving force and whose contributions to the success of the company were incalculable, died in 1921. William H. Hudson stepped into the new leadership role and the company began looking for ways to expand, modernize, and be competitive in the steamboat excursion business. The reality however was that the company already had a proven business model, which may have needed a little polish here and there, but in no way was it tarnished. In 1925 the company sold the old steamboat *Louise*.

For forty-three years *Louise* had flown the flag of the company, a big white "T" on a blue and red background, and during that time she had served the company well. A February 1925 newspaper article in the *Baltimore Sun* sadly lamented her sale and then quick departure from Baltimore waters and the Chesapeake altogether. The writer of the article estimated that she had shuttled an average of 300,000 passengers a year or 12,900,000 passengers during her tenure of crossing the Chesapeake between Baltimore and Tolchester Beach. In the same article were found these words of endearment, "*The Louise and courtship are synonymous in the minds of a good many Baltimoreans. She is a flirtation walk, a lovers' lane, a rose-scented garden, a drifting canoe, a moonlit summerhouse – all rolled into one.*" The *Louise* was known for her resonant whistle. It was widely thought that the sound of her whistle was deeper, more distinctive,

and carried further than that of any other steamboat on the Chesapeake Bay. So familiar was the *Louise's* whistle and so dependable was her schedule that many Baltimoreans were in the habit of setting their clocks and watches to her comings and goings.

The sale of the *Louise* was clearly a company blunder. Not long after the *Louise* departed Baltimore for its last time, the company realized it had made a big mistake. They had sold off the very boat that had defined the company and the Tolchester Beach excursion. Baltimoreans had loved the *Louise* and they greatly missed her when she left. She had been a Baltimore tradition, a familiar sight, and a part of the city as sure as the Shot Tower, the Bromo-Seltzer Building or the pagoda in Patterson Park. Years after she departed, many Baltimoreans still remembered their favorite steamer, the *Louise*, and her familiar whistle.

Tolchester Beach souvenir pennant.

An interesting story with a connection to the steamboat *Louise* is that of William Libby who went to work for the Tolchester Company in 1898 at the tender age of thirteen. He began his career with the company by being a candy vendor onboard the then brand-new steamer *Susquehanna*. In the years to follow he worked his way up through the company ranks as he earned first his Mate's license, then his Pilot's license, and eventually his Master's Seamanship license. In addition to the *Susquehanna*, he served on the *Annapolis*, *Emma Giles*, *Express*, *Louise*, and *Tolchester*. When it was mentioned in a 1937 newspaper article that he was poised to be the purser for the company's newly acquired vessel, the *Chelsea*, William Libby had already worked on various Tolchester steamboats for thirty-nine years. The old *Louise* must have surely been his favorite boat however, for these three reasons. First, at the time of William Libby's birth his father was serving as a live-aboard mate with his mother on the *Louise*. Second, on the *Louise*, in one of its cabins, while it was in dry-dock for repairs in 1885, William Libby had been born. Third, and years later, William Libby met his sweetheart while the *Louise* was underway on one of its trips to Tolchester Beach. Over subsequent trips the romance blossomed and eventually Libby married his sweetheart.

In 1925, the company's object of desire to replace the good ship *Louise* was a ferry boat it had found for sale in New York. To Baltimoreans, there was a stark and clear difference between the two vessels. The *Express* had none of the graceful lines and curves of the old *Louise*. Even after alterations, which added an excursion deck, the *Express* did not look at all like an excursion boat. With her two pilot houses, a length of 225 feet, and a beam of sixty-one feet, her square and boxy look showed her for what she had been built to be, a stocky automobile and truck ferryboat. With the *Express* the Tolchester Company had hoped to capture the best of both worlds, walk-on day excursionists bound for Tolchester Beach and owners of automobiles and trucks seeking a shorter way across the bay instead of having to drive around it. To this end, *Express* was a bitter disappointment, as she was not well patronized by either clientele. The *Express* was also an expensive boat to maintain and to operate. Furthermore, she was also prone to frequent breakdowns. The *Express* stopped running to Tolchester in 1933. The company was able to sell her off to be converted into a barge for a paper mill in 1937.

The company's next boat was also found in New York waters, but it looked nothing like the *Express*. The company purchased the *Bombay* and brought her to Baltimore in 1933. The *Bombay* was 260 feet in length and had a beam of sixty-four feet. *Bombay* also had the all important traditional multi-deck and big side-wheel steamboat appearance that Baltimoreans wanted to see in an excursion boat. Once it arrived at Baltimore, the vessel was renamed *Tolchester*. This was the second boat to be so named by the company. The first *Tolchester*, acquired back in 1889 as the *Samuel M. Felton*, had proven to be unsatisfactory and the company sold the boat the following year. The company put high hopes in their second *Tolchester* and they were relieved when she was embraced by Baltimoreans. This second *Tolchester* had seen much water under her keel before the Tolchester Company purchased her. Before she ended up in New York as the *Bombay*, she had been used as an excursion boat for many years on the Potomac River between Washington D.C. and Colonial Beach, Virginia, as the *St. Johns*. The *St. Johns* on the Potomac River had been as much loved as the *Louise* had been on the Chesapeake Bay.

Steamer *Tolchester. Courtesy of Tolchester Beach Revisited Museum.*

The finances of the company see-sawed, but more often teetered on the downside in the early 1930s. Finances even dipped into the red one year. The nationwide depression and the disappointing experience of the ferryboat *Express* had hit the company in the pocketbook hard and cold. With the depressed economy, boat patronage to Tolchester Beach had fallen off. Operating costs and maintenance expenditures of the *Express* had been more than the revenue she ever produced. The last of the company's river routes were abandoned because they were no longer profitable. The wharf and pier properties associated with them were sold to cut expenses and raise funds. The company had tried to turn things around by purchasing the *Bombay* (*Tolchester*), but the vessel's initial purchase price and the unforeseen early repairs it had needed had done nothing to push the company's revenues up. The company sent the *Emma Giles* to the shipyard for a quick alteration to have her bow section modified so that she could carry a half dozen or so automobiles and small trucks. The Tolchester Company sought new funding, and to get its existing loans extended or renegotiated; however, nothing worked. In February of 1935 the Tolchester Beach Improvement Company filed for bankruptcy. Legal proceedings, creditor positioning, and court papers hung like a noose around the company for two seasons and nearly two years as the company continued to operate and sought a solution to its financial woes. Then, in the fall of 1936, the noose was drawn, the end came, and the Tolchester Beach Improvement Company slipped from the scene.

In May of 1937 a new company, Tolchester Lines, Inc., took possession and control of the boats, the Light Street piers, and the Kent County property of the old Tolchester Beach Improvement Company. Having put up fifty percent of the money to make the purchase, Benjamin Bowling Wills was Tolchester Lines' largest shareholder, and became the president of the company. At this time the nation as a whole was beginning to pull itself out of the great depression. B. B. Wills was a confident and self made, successful businessman. He was optimistic and thought that under his management he could revitalize the excursion business to Tolchester Beach. Wills also thought it was the right time to revisit the previous company's idea of operating an automobile and truck ferry service between Baltimore and Tolchester Beach.

To give action to his desire to establish a ferryboat service across the Chesapeake, B. B. Wills found a big double-ended steel ferryboat available for lease from the Reading Railroad. The *Chelsea*, built in 1923, had a length of 189 feet and a beam of thirty-six feet. On December 2nd 1937, the ferryboat took its initial test run down the Patapsco River. Two days later on a Saturday it began a regular schedule of two trips per day at 7:30 a.m. and 3:00 p.m. between Baltimore and Tolchester Beach. The ultimate intention of Wills though was to build a terminal in the Bay Shore area, east of Baltimore, and establish a larger ferryboat operation connecting Bay Shore with Tolchester Beach. To this end

he sought state approval and a yearly state subsidy to offset the cost of the ferry operation, both of which he had been able to obtain on the Baltimore to Tolchester route. If he secured approval he was going to increase the number of trips to five, and he was going to upgrade the *Chelsea* to handle more vehicles. He had several different sites selected in the Bay Shore area, which are roughly ten to twelve road miles east of Baltimore.

Any of the sites he had in mind would have cut the across-the-Bay distance down from twenty-seven miles to roughly eight miles. A huge savings in fuel and operating expenses, as well as travel time, would have been realized. It was hoped that by already having a ferryboat operational between Baltimore and Tolchester that his chances of winning the state's approval for the Bay Shore to Tolchester operation would be greatly improved. It was a very bold, and at the same time, a very logical and calculating way of thinking, but the State of Maryland failed to give their approval for the Bay Shore to Tolchester ferry idea. Left with a leased ferryboat that quickly proved to be too large and too expensive to operate between Baltimore and Tolchester, Wills suspended the ferryboat service in February 1938. *Chelsea* was promptly returned to the Reading Railroad. The Bay Shore to Tolchester ferry idea surfaced again in 1943. This time though, the idea was proposed by a number of Kent County civic organizations. The organizations believed that the new ferry service would

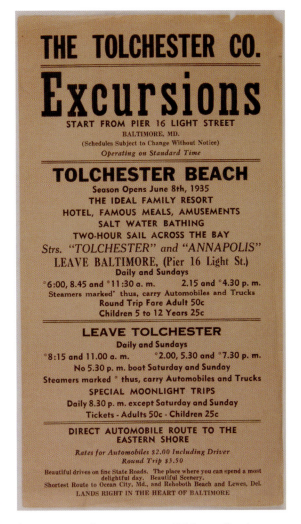

Announcement for excursions to Tolchester Beach. Season opens on June 8th, 1935. Two hour sail across the Bay aboard the steamers *Tolchester* and *Annapolis*.

revitalize and be a boon to Kent County tourism. B. B. Wills was quoted in a *Sun* newspaper article dated January 23, 1943, as saying he was willing to take on the project "*provided the people on the Eastern Shore want it.*" He also stated that the service should warrant a $25,000 per year state subsidy. The idea, however, never advanced beyond talk and a number of newspaper articles.

In November 1938, Wills was ready to revive the ferryboat service between downtown Baltimore and Tolchester. This time though he would implement a much more limited version of the plan. He brought over the *Southport* from his Potomac River operation. The *Southport* did not look like a ferryboat. She had the appearance and all the lines of a conventional steamboat. Southport was 130 feet long and had a beam of twenty-five feet. She was not very large and certainly a less than ideal vessel to ferry automobiles. Her bow railings had been cut away and her freight deck opened in the front, similar to the alterations that had been done to the *Emma Giles* and the *Annapolis*. Wills estimated that with her alterations she could carry twelve automobiles and had additional space for around 350 foot passengers. On November 23, 1938, the vessel made its initial run across the Chesapeake Bay. The *Southport* made two trips each way daily, leaving Baltimore at 8 a.m. and 3 p.m. Two and a half years later and at the start of the war, *Southport* was requisitioned by the U.S. Army. With the departure of the *Southport*, the days of the Tolchester Lines transporting automobiles and trucks between Baltimore and Tolchester became history.

Baltimoreans loved her; however, B. B. Willis was never enamored with the side-wheeler *Tolchester*. He considered the *Tolchester* an expensive boat to operate, but perhaps the actual reason was because he viewed the *Tolchester* through the filter of his *Potomac*. The *Potomac* was a massive 314-foot vessel with three towering smoke stacks that Wills was operating on the Potomac River at the time. The *Potomac* was the former *Albany* and had been built by the Hudson River Day Line in 1880. She had been built with no compromise to luxury and class; but no longer needed by the Day Line, she had not moved from a New York pier for several years when Wills spotted her. Wills was able to purchase her at an attractive price. He first used the vessel as an excursion boat between Washington, D.C. and his small and struggling amusement park and bathing beach at Chapel Point in Charles County. After Wills closed the park for lack of patronage, he continued to use *Albany*, with her two big dance floors, as a nighttime party boat for champagne toting, fun seeking Washingtonians. The *Potomac* also made periodic daytime excursions to the ever-popular bathing and summer resort of Colonial Beach, Virginia. As mentioned previously, the *Tolchester* as the former *St. Johns* had also successfully plied the same route years earlier. B. B. Wills, as the focused and careful businessman that he was, surely did not have the time to ponder or care about romantic connections such as this, however. *Tolchester* continued in her duties and performed adequately the job of escorting excursionists to and from Tolchester Beach through the

1940 season. Then just before the start of the 1941 season, on May 15th, the *Tolchester* caught fire and burned to the waterline at the company's Pier 16 on Light Street. The vessel had just undergone shipyard repairs and the exact cause of the fire was never determined.

The timing of the burning of the *Tolchester* could not have been worse. Wills had to scramble fast to find a replacement for the summer excursion season. He was able to lease and eventually purchase the steamer *Mohawk* from the Rock Creek Steamboat Company. As a boat for short trips down the Patapsco to the half dozen or so pleasure points on Rock Creek in Anne Arundel County, where speed was not an issue, she was quite satisfactory. However, for the longer jaunt to Tolchester Beach, she was underpowered. *Mohawk* was also too small to handle all of the anticipated crowds bound for Tolchester Beach that summer. *Mohawk* had been built in 1904 as the *Anne Arundel*. The vessel was 174 feet in length and could accommodate roughly 1,300 passengers. To make up for the inherent deficiencies of the *Mohawk*, Wills added a second boat, the *Francis Scott Key*. The *Francis Scott Key*, however, was no newcomer to Baltimore. She had ironically been built by the Tolchester Beach Improvement Company back in 1898 as the *Susquehanna*. The company had sold her in 1923 because she did not fit in at the time with the company's new focus on developing an across-the-Bay ferryboat operation. After being operated in New Orleans for a time and later in New York by the Sound Steamship Lines, Wills was able to purchase the *Susquehanna* in 1940. Many Baltimoreans still had warm memories of the *Susquehanna*, and they welcomed her return as the *Francis Scott Key*.

At the start of WWII *Mohawk* was requisitioned by the government and steamed south for a tour of duty in the Hampton Roads, Virginia, corner of the Chesapeake. During the war years gasoline was in short supply. The big parking lot at Tolchester rarely saw a car come or go. However, every time the *Francis Scott Key* maneuvered away from her dock at Pier 16, she left a big group of would be excursionists frustrated and disappointed. Wills also had difficulty finding persons willing to work at the park or on the boat during the war years. At one point Wills even rolled up his sleeves and did some of the manual tasks on the boat himself. Many of the park rides and concessions remained closed throughout the duration of the war for lack of hired help. For the 1942 season Wills was able to charter the *Wauketa* from the Sutton Line to assist the *Francis Scott Key*. Wills was also able to convince the government that his Tolchester Lines, across-the-Bay, operation was necessary. Where many steamship lines had to stop operating for lack of fuel during the war years—the Wilson Line that ran excursions to Seaside Park in Calvert County with their *Bay Belle* being one—Tolchester Lines continued to operate.

In 1943 B. B. Wills purchased the *Bear Mountain* from the Mandalay Line, which operated steamboats on the Hudson River. *Bear Mountain* was named for a prominent and well-known mountain in the Hudson River Valley, which resembles the profile of a bear in a lying down position. The *Bear Mountain* was 243 feet in length, had a beam of thirty-six feet, and could carry 2,100 passengers. As soon as *Bear Mountain* had completed its voyage down from New York it replaced *Wauketa* and began racking up miles of Chesapeake Bay water under its keel, transporting excursionist back and forth between Baltimore and Tolchester Beach. *Bear Mountain* performed well as an excursion boat on the Chesapeake, but many who sailed on the boat were unfamiliar with its history and were puzzled by its clearly non-Chesapeake sounding name. When the 1948 season ended, Wills transferred *Bear Mountain* to his Potomac River operation where it replaced the *Albany*.

To replace the redeployed *Bear Mountain* the Tolchester Lines in the fall of 1948 purchased the *Asbury Park* from Jersey Shore Lines of Atlantic Highlands, New Jersey. Renamed *Tolchester*, she was the third vessel to be so named, and the second Tolchester Lines boat to have the honor. The *Tolchester* had a length of 198 feet and a beam of forty-four feet. *Tolchester* began making the across-the-Bay trips to Tolchester Beach in 1949. The vessel had originally been built as the *City of Philadelphia* for the Wilson Line back in 1910. In 1938 the Wilson Line sent the vessel to the shipyard to have everything above its hull rebuilt new. To save money, the company did not change her engines. After conversion the vessel had a distinctly modernistic and streamlined appearance and was renamed *Liberty Belle*. The new *Liberty Belle* was proclaimed by Wilson Line as "*The world's first river stream-liner.*" The Wilson Line further described *Liberty Belle* as having "*Scores of luxury liner features. 2,500 passenger capacity. Special observation bridge and a glass enclosed pilot house.*" The Wilson Line used *Liberty Belle* as a dance and party boat on the Delaware River and Bay. *Liberty Belle* would leave from Philadelphia at 4:30 p.m. and Wilmington at 7 p.m. She was also used during the summer months for special excursions.

In April 1942 the Navy acquired the *Liberty Belle* from the Wilson Line and as the *USS Liberty Belle* (IX-72) she rode out the war years assigned to the Naval Mine Warfare Test Station at Solomons, Maryland. No longer needed by the Navy after the war, the vessel was offered back to the Wilson Line but they refused her because of her deteriorated condition. Instead she was sold to Jersey Shore Lines, which renamed her *Asbury Park* and put her back in good working order. During the regular season in the early 1950s the *Tolchester* left Pier 5, Pratt Street bound for Tolchester Beach at 9:30 a.m. and returned at 7:00 p.m. It was a leisurely two-hour boat ride between Baltimore and Tolchester Beach, which meant excursionists had around five hours to do as they desired at the park. On Sundays and holidays, the *Tolchester* departed Baltimore at 8:30 a.m., 2:30 p.m., and 7:30 p.m. The boat also departed Tolchester Beach at three different times, the latest being 9:45 p.m. with arrival at the Pratt Street pier at 11:45 p.m. The adult round trip fare for day trips was $1.25. For children the cost was sixty-five cents. Moonlight round trips were more affordable, $1.15 for an adult and a mere fifty cents for a child.

Since the end of WWII the Tolchester Lines had a competitor in the across-the-Bay excursion boat business. That competitor was the Wilson Line and the boat was the *Bay Belle*. The Wilson Line had operated a highly successful excursion to Seaside Park in Calvert County for a number of years before the war. However, the company had been forced to curtail the boat trips to Seaside Park in 1942 because of mandatory fuel rationing. At war's end, the Wilson Line looked to revive the service but was unable to do so because the pier at Seaside Park had deteriorated beyond repair during its time of disuse. The Wilson Line then looked at Betterton, found the pier there to be in better shape, and in June 1946 began offering excursions between Baltimore and that beach resort. With two boat lines, each proclaiming to be the best, and with two beach resorts in close proximity to one another, many excursionists had a difficult time choosing between a cruise to Betterton onboard the *Bay Belle* or a cruise to Tolchester Beach onboard the *Tolchester*. To the untrained eye, both vessels looked very much the same. They looked to be the same length and both had four big decks. Each boat had a backward slanting funnel, and with other details, presented a streamlined appearance. However, the two boats were distinguishable from each other. The primary difference was that the pilothouse of the *Bay Belle* had a curved look to it while that of the *Tolchester* had a straighter and more squared off look.

It is interesting that the *Bay Belle* and the *Tolchester* were operating in direct competition with one another. For many years earlier, the two vessels had been built as sister ships, both having been built to the same specifications. When the vessels had first been launched back in November 1909, the only way to tell them apart was by their nameplates. The two vessels had been launched on the same day and only fourteen minutes apart from one another. They had been built at the Harlan & Hollingworth shipyard in Wilmington, Delaware. The Wilson line had contracted for their construction. *Bay Belle* had originally been built as the *City of Wilmington*, official number 207202. As mentioned earlier, *Tolchester* had been built as the *City of Philadelphia*, official number 207201.

In 1951 the Tolchester Lines moved its base of operations from Light Street to Pier 5 on Pratt Street. The change had been necessitated by the City of Baltimore widening Light Street to improve traffic flow and modernizing the harbor area primarily for aesthetic reasons. All the old steamboat offices and piers along the entire length of Light Street were torn down. Tolchester Lines received $56,000 in compensation from the city for their Light Street property. Growth and change in general accelerated greatly in the 1950s. The way people socialized and sought entertainment was no exception, the primary driver behind this change being the automobile. By the mid-1950s automobiles had become faster, more comfortable, more reliable, and more affordable. Add improved roads, bridges, and interstate highways, and America by the mid-1950s had truly become the land of the mobile via the great American automobile. Television also had a huge effect on how people spent their leisure hours. To be entertained it was no longer necessary for one to go to the theatre, the park, the beach, or even sit on the front steps. Entertainment came right into the home via the box in the corner of the living room with the rabbit ears. Automobiles and televisions in a sense did away with the necessity for people to partake in activities together in big groups or even in smaller family groups. For the most part, by the mid-1950s people had ceased doing things in the big group way as they had done earlier. Suddenly, going to a place like Tolchester Beach was something that mom and dad used to do, or grandpa and grandma had done years ago, but surely nothing one did today. When a family said it was going to the beach, they did not mean taking a ride on a steamboat across the Bay to Tolchester Beach. It was implied that dad was going to drive the big Chevy or Ford V8 with tail fins and lots of flashy chrome across the Bay Bridge and all the way to Ocean City or Rehoboth Beach. All of these changes had a profound effect upon companies in the steamboat excursion business.

The S. S. Tolchester underway, July 1956. *Courtesy of the Steamship Historical Society of America, Inc.*

In the spring of 1957, Tolchester Lines and Wilson Lines came to an agreement to work together on the Chesapeake. The partnership was formed out of necessity as there was no longer enough patronage for the two companies to continue to operate in competition with each other. The agreement speci-

fied that the Wilson Line's *Bay Belle* was to stop at the pier at Tolchester Beach before heading on to Betterton. At Betterton *Bay Belle* would lay over a few hours. On the way back to Baltimore *Bay Belle* would again pause at Tolchester Beach to pick up passengers. The Tolchester Line's *Tolchester* would be used as a relief boat and also for special excursions. The partnership between the two companies lasted only one season. In 1958 Tolchester Lines sold their Tolchester Beach property to a newly organized company, the Wilson-Tolchester Steamship Company. This new company had no ties to either the Wilson Line or to Tolchester Lines, but was instead associated with a Maryland bus company.

Tolchester Lines, still under the management of B. B. Wills, transferred the *Tolchester* to the Potomac River. Wills promptly leased the vessel to a group of investors who renamed it *Freestone*. They fitted the vessel out with rows of slot machines and tied her up to a pier on the Virginia side of the Potomac. The state of Virginia had strict anti-gambling laws at the time but the waters of the Potomac were under Maryland jurisdiction. For Virginians eager to pull the handles of the one-armed bandits (slot machines), all they had to do was walk to the end of the pier and step onto the boat for the pleasure to begin. The gambling boat venture however was short-lived, for in 1958 the Maryland legislature tightened its slot machine law to forbid them from any establishment which could not be reached from Maryland soil. At about the same time that the Tolchester Lines suspended its operations on the Chesapeake, the Wilson Line suspended theirs; they leased their *Bay Belle* to the new owners of Tolchester Beach.

By the 1960s, Tolchester Beach was in its final and declining years as a beach resort. Ownership of the park would change hands two more time before the park closed for good. During the summer of 1960 newspaper advertisements read as follows: "*Enjoy a Day of Fun for ALL, SAIL ABOARD THE S. S. BAY BELLE. Ideal for family or group outings. Bargain days at Tolchester Park, $2.00 in ride tickets for $1.00 with this advertisement.*" Unlike in the past though, the public at large was no longer wooed by such ads. The across-the-Bay excursion boat ride and Tolchester Beach itself had lost their charm. Interest in the rolling blue ocean surf and the boardwalk lifestyles to be had at Ocean City, Rehoboth Beach, and neighboring beaches was at an all time high. The slogan "*down the ocean*" was coined.

On Saturday October 20, 1962, at two p.m., the fifty two acres fronting on the Chesapeake Bay known as Tolchester Beach and improved with a hotel, bathing pavilion, excursion house, picnic groves, assorted amusement buildings, and a steamboat pier were sold at a bankruptcy sale for the sum of $75,000. There were a number of watchers but only one hand in the air at the "on site" sale that day. The sole bidder, the purchaser of the property, was the mortgage holder. At the time of the bankruptcy sale, most adult Baltimoreans could still recount vivid and fond memories of Tolchester Beach from the days of their youth, but few of those Baltimoreans were probably even aware that

Tolchester Beach was headed toward a rendezvous with the auction gavel. The summer of 1961 had been the park's last. For the past half dozen or so years before that, the park had just limped along, refusing to die, as different owners reminisced over its halcyon days and tried to grasp the viability of its future. A newspaper article, reporting on the sale the day after, recounted a short history of the amusement park and bathing beach. Tolchester Beach was summed up as follows: *"the grand old beach for generations of Baltimoreans."* A true statement and a poignant statement it was, for indeed Tolchester Beach had been one of, if not the largest resort and bathing beach on the Chesapeake Bay. She had also been revered by generations of Baltimoreans.

All through 1962 Tolchester Beach had sat vacant and deserted. After the bankruptcy sale, it remained neglected and largely overlooked for half a dozen more years. Of course vandals, salvage hunters, and souvenir seekers made their rounds. The windows and doors of buildings were either smashed or removed completely. Roofs decayed and collapsed under their own weight. Walkways soon became impassable due to shore grass, weeds, and briar bushes. The beach became cluttered with washed in seaweed and driftwood, along with a sampling of things that could be lost or thrown from a boat and float on a wave such as beer and soda bottles, broken ski lines, crab floats, empty quart size outboard motor oil containers, life preserver vests, and boat bailers fashioned from empty Clorox containers. A fire of unknown origin destroyed the old hotel one day. Then over the winter of 1969 and 1970 a bulldozer began rearranging the landscape. What hadn't already burned or fallen into itself was helped along through controlled burning. Like so many other amusement park places once situated around the Chesapeake Bay tidewater region—Bay Shore Park, Bay Ridge, Beverly Beach, River View Park, and Seaside Park to name just a few—the final end had come for Tolchester Beach.

Thankfully memories persist and we have faded photographs and old postcards to remind, but today at Tolchester there is no trace of the beach resort. A historical marker assures the sentimental driver with camera that the right spot has been found. Most of the traffic, however, consists of the occasional car or truck, sometimes with a trailer attached, having business at the boat marina now occupying a portion of the old Tolchester Beach resort site.

S. S. Bay Belle pin. Circa 1950s.

S. S. Tolchester pin. Circa 1950s.

ABOUT POSTCARD VALUES

An estimate of value has been assigned to each postcard in this book. That value is located at the end of each postcard's caption line. Postcard values are an estimate only. Pricing postcards is a very subjective matter. Normally the price asked for a postcard is higher when it is being offered for sale in the same area that the postcard represents. Also postcards from certain parts of the country sell better than other areas, consequently their prices will be higher. The price offered for a postcard generally varies depending on the type of environment in which it is being offered for sale. A postcard being offered for sale from an unsorted box at a flea market will generally cost less than an identical postcard at a postcard show where postcards are displayed better and organized into specific categories. Specialty postcard dealers can and do get more for their postcards because they have their pulse on the market. They understand which postcards are desirable and which are not. By handling lots of postcards, they are able to distinguish the rare from the common, and the postcards that fall in between. Rare postcards from an area where no one collects are worth less than more common postcards from an area where there are many collectors. The collector base for an area is constantly changing as individuals enter and exit the marketplace. Therefore prices do not always go up; sometimes they stabilize at a certain level for a long time or even go down.

DETERMINING THE AGE OF POSTCARDS

The following is a chronological list of the major postcard eras and the characteristic style of each era.

Pioneer Era (1893-1898) – These are postcards mailed before the Private Mailing Card Act of 1898. The postcards had illustrations either printed on government issued postal cards or privately printed souvenir cards. The government postal cards included pre-printed postage of one cent. A two-cent stamp was required for the privately printed souvenir cards.

Private Mailing Card Era (1898-1901) – The backside of the postcard has "Private Mailing Card" printed on it. The backside was for the recipient's address only. Any handwritten message will be found on the front side.

Undivided Back Postcard Era (1902-1907) – The wording "Postcard" is printed on the backside. The backside was for the recipient's address only.

Divided Back Era (1907-1914) – Postcards were produced by a high quality chromolithographic process using at least six different inks. In addition to the address area, the backside of the postcards had a space to the left where a message could be written.

White Border Era (1915-1930) – The backside has a divided back to accommodate both the recipient's address and a short message from the sender. The front of the postcard has a white border around the entire image.

Linen Era (1930-1950) – Postcards were made with a high rag, linen type paper with a textured feel. The images found on linen postcards tend to be highly stylized and typically look more impressive than reality.

Photochrome (Chrome) Era (1950 to mid-1970s) – These postcards have a glossy surface and are made from color photos. They are similar in appearance, but are not actual photos. The images are generally sharp and well composed.

Continental (Modern) Era (mid-1970s to date) – These are similar in appearance to postcards from the photochrome era but they are a larger size of 4 x 6 inches.

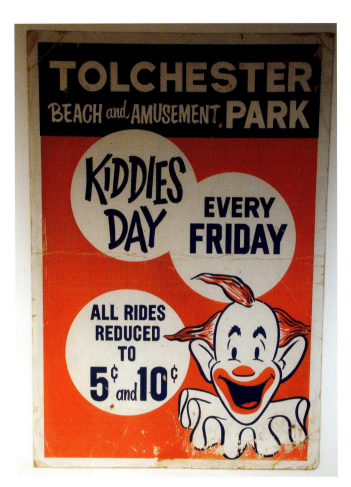

Poster announcing that every Friday was Kiddies Day at Tolchester Beach. Circa 1950s. *Courtesy of Tolchester Beach Revisited Museum.*

The Café sits neglected after the park closed. Circa 1960s. *Courtesy of Tolchester Beach Revisited Museum.*

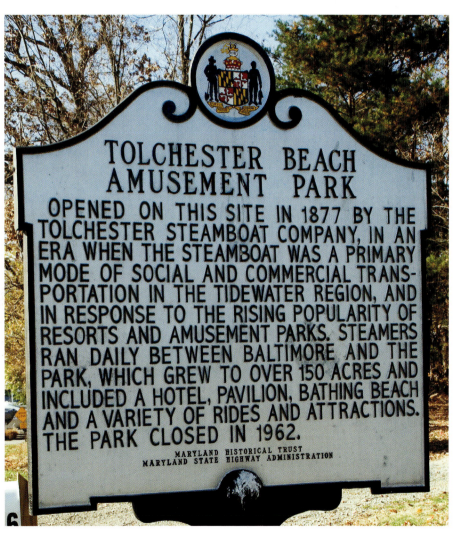

TOLCHESTER BEACH AMUSEMENT PARK

OPENED ON THIS SITE IN 1877 BY THE TOLCHESTER STEAMBOAT COMPANY, IN AN ERA WHEN THE STEAMBOAT WAS A PRIMARY MODE OF SOCIAL AND COMMERCIAL TRANSPORTATION IN THE TIDEWATER REGION, AND IN RESPONSE TO THE RISING POPULARITY OF RESORTS AND AMUSEMENT PARKS. STEAMERS RAN DAILY BETWEEN BALTIMORE AND THE PARK, WHICH GREW TO OVER 150 ACRES AND INCLUDED A HOTEL, PAVILION, BATHING BEACH AND A VARIETY OF RIDES AND ATTRACTIONS. THE PARK CLOSED IN 1962.

MARYLAND HISTORICAL TRUST
MARYLAND STATE HIGHWAY ADMINISTRATION

Historical marker at Tolchester Beach.

POSTCARDS OF BETTERTON

Bathing scene at Betterton. Circa 1907-12; $8

Scene at Betterton showing the Hotel Rigbie in the distance. Circa 1907-12; $8

Water Front showing Turners Pier.
Postmarked 1911; $8

Steamer *Susquehanna* discharging passengers at Betterton. Circa 1907-12; $10

Skating Rink and Excursion Pier. Postmarked 1910; $12

One of the fast Ericsson steamers landing at Betterton. Postmarked 1910; $10

Ericsson steamer and pier. Postmarked 1911; $10

Steamer *Penn* arriving at the Ericsson Pier. Circa 1907-12; $8

Arrival of the steamer *Penn*. Handwritten message on the backside reads: "Having a dandy time. Wish you were here." Postmarked 1912; $10

Steamer *Lord Baltimore* at Betterton. Handwritten message on the backside reads: "We are at Betterton today. This is the boat that brought us here." Postmarked 1914; $15

The Chesapeake Hotel on the beach. Dated 1909; $10

Bathing scene at Betterton. Circa 1907-09; $10

The Rigbie Hotel. Handwritten message on the backside reads: "This is a very nice hotel. Had my meals and very nice. Writing this alongside of a lonesome girl who looks like she needs someone to comfort her." Postmarked 1908; $8

The Skating Rink at Betterton. Handwritten message on the backside reads: "Have made up to stay a few days longer. That is the reason I didn't come home Saturday." Postmarked 1909; $15

Steamer *Susquehanna* at Betterton. Handwritten message on the backside reads: "Dearie why don't you write. I am on my vacation. I am having a grand time. I am here for two weeks. Please write me c/o Owen's Cottage, Betterton, Md." Postmarked 1911; $8

The launch harbor. Postmarked 1910; $15

Steamer *Susquehanna* landing at Betterton. Handwritten message on the backside reads: "This is a fine resort. We are going further down the bay each day. The Chesapeake waterways are perfectly beautiful. I wish you were with us. We are great sailors by this time. Love, Mary". Postmarked 1908; $8

Watching the bathers at Betterton. Postmarked 1907; $10

Bathing scene. Postmarked 1911; $10

Camping Scene. Postmarked 1905; $12

The harbor at Betterton. Postmarked 1905; $10

Enjoying the beach at Betterton. Dated 1907; $20

Bird's-eye view of Betterton Wharf and Chesapeake Haven in the distance.
Postmarked 1909; $10

The pier and Ericsson Line steamer.
Circa 1905-07; $12

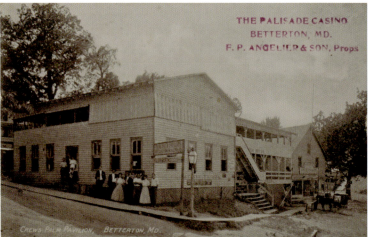

Crew's Palm Pavilion. Overprinted: "The Palisade Casino"
Postmarked 1908; $25

Ericsson Pier. Handwritten message on the backside reads: "Having a fine time but am so sunburned can nearly move." Postmarked 1908; $8

Ericsson Pier. Postmarked 1906; $10

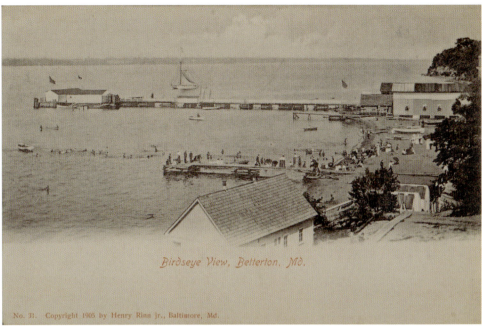

Bird's-eye view. Circa 1905-07; $12

The Chesapeake Hotel. Circa 1907-12; $8

Ericsson Pier and steamer. Circa 1907-12; $10

The beach. Postmarked 1906; $10

A side view of the Chesapeake Hotel.
Postmarked 1905; $10

The Chesapeake Hotel.
Circa 1907-12; $10

The Rigbie Hotel. Postmarked 1906; $10

The Idlewhile Cottage.
Postmarked 1906; $10

The New Belmont. Handwritten message on the backside reads: "Albert and I went fishing and caught two fish and divided up for supper." Postmarked 1909; $15

The Shadylawn Cottage. Postmarked 1908; $12

The Idlewhile Cottage. Handwritten message on the backside reads: "This is a fine place." Postmarked 1909; $8

Hotel Idlewhile. Postmarked 1911; $10

The Emerson. Postmarked 1909; $10

Price Cottage. Handwritten message on the backside: "Having a dandy time, plenty of water." Postmarked 1910; $10

Hotel Rigbie. Postmarked 1907; $12

The Idlewhile. Circa 1905-07; $12

Crew's Cottage.
Circa 1907-12; $12

The Idlewhile. Postmarked 1913; $15

The Ferncliffe. Handwritten message on the backside reads: "Am having a dandy time. Wish you were here." Postmarked 1911; $12

The Ellwood Cottage. Handwritten message on the backside reads: "I love my home but O, you Betterton. This is where we are stopping." Postmarked 1909; $15

Hotel Rigbie Hotel. Circa 1907-12; $10

The Ferncliffe Cottage. Postmarked 1909; $15

The Roselawn Cottage. Postmarked 1909; $15

The Ferncliff. Postmarked 1907; $15

Where we meet. Postmarked 1906; $8

The Hotel Chesapeake (East View). Handwritten message on the backside reads: "Am having a nice time and will have a nicer time when you come down." Postmarked 1910; $10

Camping at Betterton. Postmarked 1908; $12

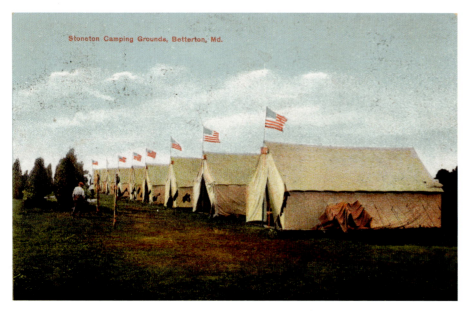

The Stoneton Camping Grounds. Postmarked 1909; $12

Arrivals at Betterton Wharf. Circa 1907-12; $8

American Hunting and Fishing Clubs Camp. Postmarked 1908; $15

Boats coming to Betterton. Postmarked 1909; $8

Bathing scene. Postmarked 1907; $7

"THE IDLEWHILE"
BETTERTON, MARYLAND
ON CHESAPEAKE BAY

Betterton Md
Aug. 30. 05.
Dear Bese
I will leave here
for Washington
to morrow after.
noon. Will be
in W- some time
Thursday eve. I don't know what
time.
Mabel.

The Idlewhile. Postmarked 1905; $12

BATHING SHORE, BETTERTON, MD.

The bathing shore. Circa 1905-07; $8

Betterton Pier and Steamer Susquehanna, Betterton, Md.

Betterton Pier and steamer *Susquehanna*. Postmarked 1907; $8

Hotel Chesapeake and bathing beach. Postmarked 1909; $8

Idlewhile Park and shore. Postmarked 1907; $8

Bathing and boating. Postmarked 1907; $8

On the boardwalk. Postmarked 1906; $10

Greetings from camp. Postmarked 1906; $15

Looking towards the shore. Postmarked 1905; $8

The log cabin. Circa 1905-07; $15

The Idlewhile Spring. Postmarked 1905; $15

45

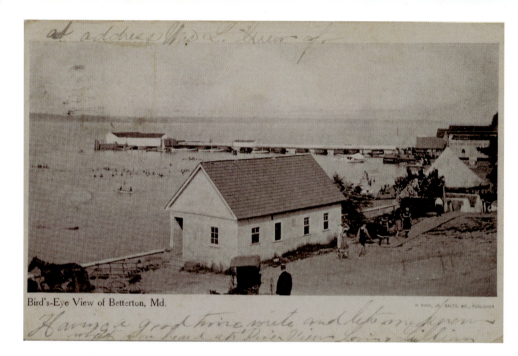

Bird's-Eye View of Betterton, Md.

Bird's-eye view of Betterton.
Postmarked 1909; $10

5 The Steamer Susquehanna at Betterton Wharf, Betterton, Md.

Ericson Pier and Steamer, Betterton, Md.

Ericsson Pier and steamer. Postmarked 1912; $12

The steamer *Susquehanna* at
Betterton Wharf. Postmarked
1907; $10

Bathing scene. Postmarked 1905; $10

Betterton Square. Postmarked 1908; $8

The park. Postmarked 1907; $10

Betterton beach. Postmarked 1909; $8

The Chesapeake Hotel.
Circa 1905; $10

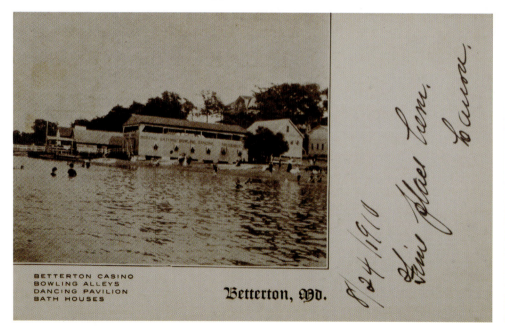

The Betterton Casino. Postmarked 1910; $15

A view from the Rigbie Hotel. Postmarked 1910; $10

Bathing scene. Postmarked 1907; $10

Hotel Ericsson. Postmarked 1906; $10

Launches at Betterton. Postmarked 1909; $10

The Emerson. Postmarked 1910; $15

Hotel Rigbie. Postmarked 1912; $10

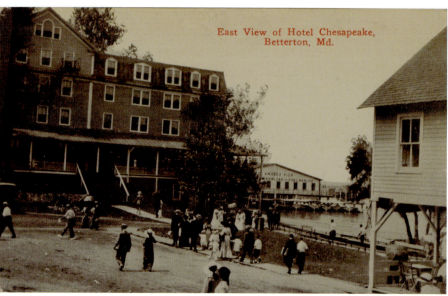

East view of Hotel Chesapeake. Postmarked 1914; $12

A view of the Ericsson Pier and the Betterton Pier.
Postmarked 1905; $20

The Boardwalk. Postmarked 1916; $30

The Emerson. Postmarked 1908; $12

Price Cottage. Postmarked 1908; $10

Owens Cottage. Circa 1907-12; $10

Hotel Betterton. Circa 1907-12; $8

Hotel Ericsson. Postmarked 1908; $12

The Price Cottage. Postmarked 1906; $12

Owens Cottage. Postmarked 1911; $110

The Rigbie Hotel. Postmarked 1906; $10

Hotel Betterton. Postmarked 1910; $10

The Belmont Cottage. Circa 1907-12; $10

The Chesapeake House. Circa 1907-12; $10

Betterton beach from the water. Postmarked 1909; $10

The Betterton Wharf. Circa 1905; $10

Bathing scene. Postmarked 1905; $8

The Shadylawn Cottage. Postmarked 1911; $15

Steamer *Susquehanna*. Handwritten message on the backside reads: "Spending a week at this place; having a grand time." Postmarked 1908; $10

Ericsson Pier and steamer. Postmarked 1904; $12

Ericsson Pier at moonlight. Postmarked 1910; $10

Boating at Betterton. Circa 1910; $10

Chesapeake Avenue looking toward Chesapeake Bay. Circa 1920s; $8

The bathing beach. Circa 1920s; $8

Bathing Beach and Amusement Pier. Circa 1920s; $8

Chesapeake Hotel and bathing beach. Postmarked 1929; $8

Beach and Skating Rink. Circa 1920s; $10

Camping Grounds. Circa 1920s; $8

The Chesapeake Hotel. Postmarked 1928; $8

Bathing scene, showing Hotel Chesapeake, Hotel Rigbie, and Turner's Pier. Postmarked 1924; $8

Bathing Beach and Amusement Pier. Postmarked 1930; $8

Sassafras River along Bayside Shore. Postmarked 1925; $8

Bathing beach. Circa 1916-25; $10

View of the piers and bay. Handwritten message on the backside reads:
"Having a lovely and quiet vacation." Postmarked 1930; $8

Business section. Circa 1920s; $8

Camping on Sassafras River shore at Betterton. Postmarked 1927; $8

Bathing beach and dance hall. Handwritten message on the backside reads: "Am having a swell time. Some swimming down here." Postmarked 1928; $8

Excursion steamer arriving at Betterton. Handwritten message on the backside reads: "Am here for awhile, children are having a great time, may want to stay longer. Postmarked 1930; $8

View of the piers and harbor. Circa 1920s; $8

Hotel Betterton. Handwritten message on the backside reads: "Enjoying the stay very much. Weather fine." Postmarked 1928; $10

Feeling in great shape at Betterton. Postmarked 1928; $6

The Idlewhile. Circa 1920s; $10

The only bit of shade on the beach. Circa 1920s; $6

Washed ashore at Betterton. Postmarked 1930; $6

Crew's Hotel. Handwritten message on the backside reads: "I am down here for a week for a quiet time. Wish you were here with me." Postmarked 1917; $10

Perfectly happy at Betterton. Postmarked 1928; $6

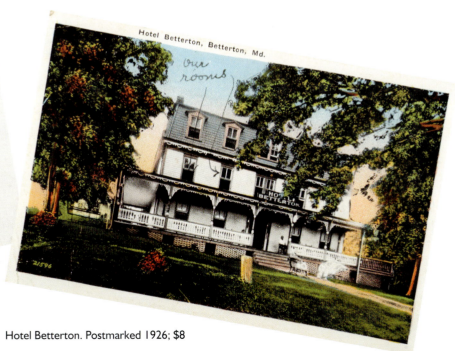

Hotel Betterton. Postmarked 1926; $8

The Price Cottage. Circa 1920s; $12

The Jewell Cottage. Circa 1916-25; $10

The Emerson. Circa 1916-25; $12

Owens Cottage and Annex. Circa 1920s; $10

The Maryland Cottage. Handwritten message on the backside reads: "Am spending my second week here. Having a nice time." Postmarked 1930; $8

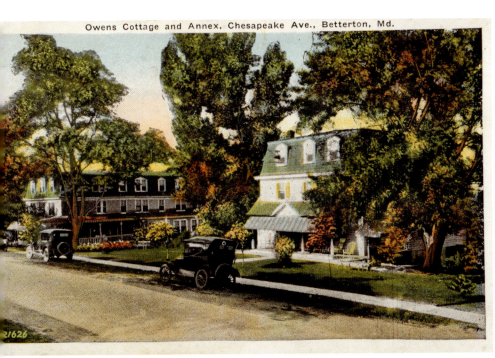

Owens Cottage and Annex, Chesapeake Avenue. Circa 1920s; $10

The Bayside Inn. Circa 1920s; $8

The Rigbie Hotel. Handwritten message on the backside reads: "It is a beautiful place and fine view of the Chesapeake and good eats." Postmarked 1933; $10

PRICE'S COTTAGE, BETTERTON, MD.

Price's Cottage. Circa 1920s; $8

HOTEL BETTERTON, BETTERTON, MD.

The Hotel Betterton. Handwritten message on the backside reads: "Here is true southern fashion. No one works hard, nor yet plays hard. Eating and sleeping and gossiping are the chief recreations and to them one becomes easily acclimated." Postmarked 1922; $10

The Southern, Betterton, Md.

The Southern. Circa 1920s; $12

HOTEL BELMONT, BETTERTON, MD.

The Hotel Belmont. Circa 1916-25; $12

The Hotel Rigbie. Circa 1920s; $10

The Maryland. Circa 1916-25; $12

The Jewell Cottage. Handwritten message on the backside reads: "It sure is grand here, such bathing, arrived at 3 a.m. Grand moonlight ride." Postmarked 1921; $10

The Atlantic. Circa 1916-25; $12

Automobile square. Circa 1920s; $15

The automobile square and the Chesapeake Hotel. Circa 1916-25; $15

The parking space at the foot of Chesapeake Avenue, showing Hotel Rigbie. Postmarked 1936; $15

Bathing beach looking towards Tolchester and Pleasure Piers. Handwritten message on the backside reads: "Having a fine time. Wish you were here." Postmarked 1928; $8

Sassafras Avenue. Postmarked 1939; $10

Daily dozen health exercises on the beach.
Postmarked 1923; $20

Ericsson Line Pier and Steamer. Circa 1916-25; $10

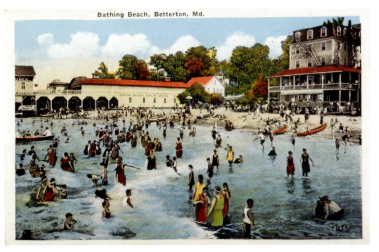

The bathing beach. Circa 1920s; $8

CHESAPEAKE HOTEL AND BATHING BEACH, BETTERTON, MD.

Chesapeake Hotel and bathing beach. Postmarked 1924; $8

ERICSSON LINE PIER, BETTERTON, MD.

The Ericsson Line Pier. Postmarked 1922; $12

HOMEWARD BOUND, BETTERTON, MD.

Homeward bound. Handwritten message on the backside reads:
"The weather and everything is fine. We are having a real good time."
Postmarked 1921; $12

VIEW FROM BAYSIDE COTTAGES, BETTERTON, MD.

View of bayside cottages. Circa 1920s; $8

The Tolchester Wharf and boat. Circa 1920s; $10

The bathing beach. Circa 1916-25; $10

The Catholic church at Betterton. Circa 1916-25; $8

The Methodist church at Betterton. Circa 1916-25; $8

View from Lovers' Leap, showing bathers ready for a dip. Circa 1916-25; $10

View of the beach from the hotels.
Circa 1920s; $8

View of the piers and Bay. Circa 1916-25; $10

Scene at the foot of Chesapeake Avenue. Circa 1920s; $10

Pleasure yachts at Betterton. Postmarked 1921; $8

The Rigbie Hotel. Circa 1920s; $10

The Philadelphia steamer arriving at Betterton. Circa 1916-25; $10

The Chesapeake Hotel. Circa 1920s; $8

Boating and bathing. Handwritten message on the backside reads: "Arrived safely and weather is fine. Will go fishing tomorrow morning if it is nice." Postmarked 1938; $8

Bathing hour at Betterton. Handwritten message on the backside reads: "This is a very pretty place and I am having a pleasant time." Postmarked 1917; $8

The bathing beach. Postmarked 1924; $8

Water scene at Betterton. Circa 1930s-40s; $7

The boardwalk. Postmarked 1944; $7

Hotel Betterton. Handwritten message on the backside reads: "Here I am having a lazy life, which is just what I need. The weather has been perfect for the beach." Postmarked 1945; $7

HOTEL CHESAPEAKE OVERLOOKING CHESAPEAKE BAY, BETTERTON, MD.

Hotel Chesapeake overlooking the Chesapeake Bay. Handwritten message on the backside reads: "Just arrived but have taken in almost everything." Postmarked 1940; $8

BETTERTON BATHING BEACH
BETTERTON, MD.

24208

AERIAL VIEW, BEATTY'S AMUSEMENT PIER AND BEACH

Photo by Eliason Photographic Service, Chestertown, Md.

BETTERTON BEACH, MARYLAND

Betterton's bathing beach. Handwritten message on the backside reads: "We are staying at the Chesapeake Hotel. We had nice adjoining rooms but they changed their minds and now we have rooms across the hall. I've unpacked all my things again." Postmarked 1942; $7

Aerial view of Beatty's Amusement Pier. Circa 1940s-50s; $7

BEATTY'S AMUSEMENT PIER, SURF CLUB AND BATHING BEACH

BETTERTON BEACH, MARYLAND

Beatty's Amusement Pier, Surf Club, and bathing beach. Circa 1940s-50s; $7

AERIAL VIEW, BEATTY'S AMUSEMENT PIER AND BEACH

Photo by Eliason Photographic Service, Chestertown, Md.

BETTERTON BEACH, MARYLAND

BEATTY'S SURF CLUB

BETTERTON BEACH, MARYLAND

Beatty's Surf Club.
Circa 1940s-50s; $7

Aerial view of Beatty's Amusement Pier and beach. Printed message on the backside reads: "Daily excursions on the *Bay Belle* leaves from the Wilson Line Pier in Baltimore for a delightful three hour cruise up the Chesapeake Bay to Betterton or can be reached by automobile." Circa 1940s-50s; $7

Greetings from
Betterton, Maryland.
Circa 1940s-50s; $7

Printed message on the backside reads: "Cottages at Evergreen Knoll. Rentals weekly and monthly." Circa 1940s-50s; $7

The pier and amusement center. Circa 1940s-50s; $7

2—Bathing Beach and Pier, Betterton Md. on the Chesapeake Bay

6B-H2057

Bathing beach and pier. Circa 1940s-50s; $7

3—Bathing Beach and Chesapeake Hotel, Betterton, Md. on the Chesapeake Bay

6B-H2058

Bathing beach and Chesapeake Hotel. Circa 1940s-50s; $7

4—Hotel Betterton, Betterton, Md. on the Chesapeake Bay

6B-H2059

The Hotel Betterton.
Circa 1940s-50s; $7

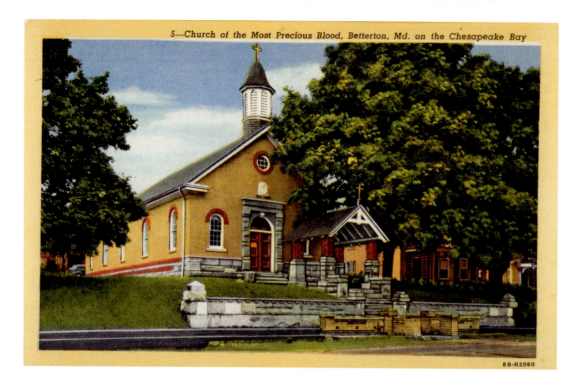

5—Church of the Most Precious Blood, Betterton, Md. on the Chesapeake Bay

Church of the Most Precious Blood. Circa 1940s-50s; $7

6—Fleetwood House, Betterton, Md. on the Chesapeake Bay

The Fleetwood House. Circa 1940s-50s; $7

7—Hotel Rigbie, Betterton, Md. on the Chesapeake Bay

The Hotel Rigbie. Circa 1940s-50s; $7

78

The S. S. *Bay Belle*. Daily cruises from Baltimore to Betterton. Circa 1940s-50s; $7

The Chesapeake Hotel. Circa 1940s-50s; $7

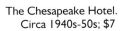

Becker's Beach Club and bathing beach. Circa 1940s-50s; $7

Betterton beach
and boat pier. Circa
1940s-50s; $7

Betterton beach view of Betterton. Circa 1940s-50s; $7

The Hotel Chesapeake and Cottages. Circa 1940s-50s; $7

SCENE FROM HOTEL RIGBIE PORCH, BETTERTON, MD.

Scene from the Hotel Rigbie porch. Handwritten message on the backside reads: "Fine weather, water smooth as glass." Postmarked 1939; $7

HOTEL RIGBIE AND PIER, BETTERTON, MD.

The Hotel Rigbie and pier. Postmarked 1943; $15

HOTEL RIGBIE AND PART OF BEACH, BETTERTON, MD.

The Hotel Rigbie and part of the beach. Circa 1940s; $12

HOTEL RIGBIE FROM CHESAPEAKE BAY, BETTERTON, MD.

The Hotel Rigbie from the Chesapeake Bay. Circa 1940s-50s; $7

The Ferncliffe Hotel. Circa 1940s-50s; $7

FERNCLIFFE HOTEL, BETTERTON, MD.

MOTOR VESSEL
PORT WELCOME
CRUISING ON CHESAPEAKE BAY

The *M. V. Port Welcome*: the last
excursion boat to call at Betterton.
Circa 1960s; $7

The Royal Swan Hotel.
Circa 1940s; $7

ROYAL SWAN HOTEL, BETTERTON, MD.

POSTCARDS OF TOLCHESTER BEACH

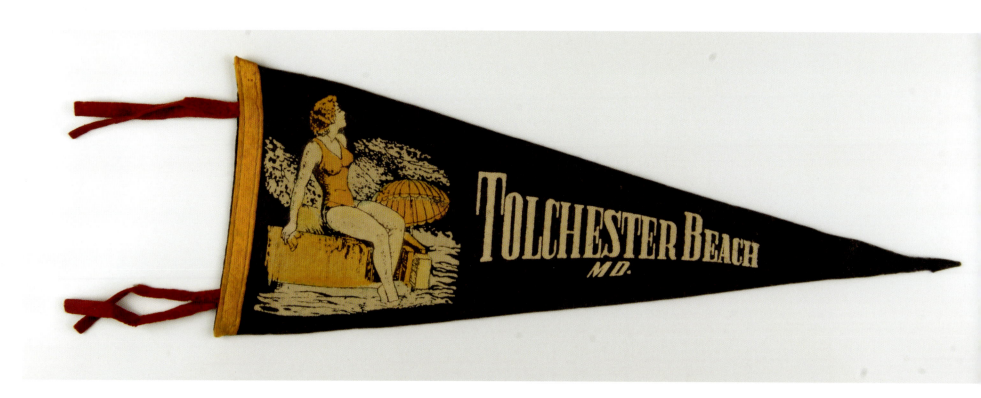

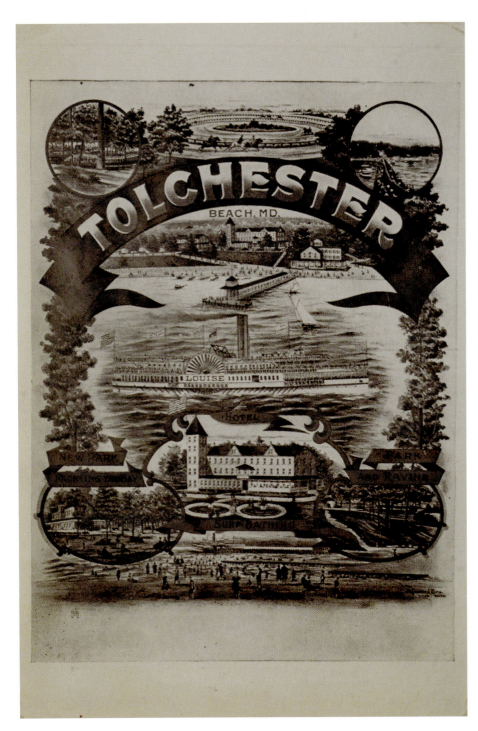

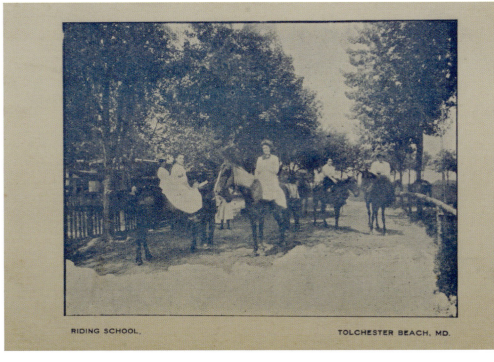

Riding school at Tolchester Beach. Postmarked 1911; $20

Scenes at Tolchester Beach.
Circa 1907; $20

GOAT TRACK,

TOLCHESTER BEACH, MD.

The goat track at Tolchester Beach. Circa 1907-12; $20

THE GREAT PIKES PEAKE,   TOLCHESTER BEACH, MD.

ANNEX HOTEL.   TOLCHESTER BEACH, MD.

The Great Pikes Peak at Tolchester Beach. Circa 1907-12; $20

The Annex Hotel at Tolchester Beach. Handwritten message on the backside reads: "We had a grand time today." Postmarked 1911; $20

LADIES AND GENTS RETIRING ROOM,   TOLCHESTER BEACH, MD.

The ladies and gents retiring room at Tolchester Beach. Postmarked 1911; $20

PENNY PARLOR, POSTALS, SHELLS, ETC.   TOLCHESTER BEACH, MD.

Penny Parlor, postals, shells, etc. at Tolchester Beach. Postmarked 1910; $20

TICKLER,   TOLCHESTER BEACH, MD.

The Tickler at Tolchester Beach. Handwritten message on the backside reads: "I was at Tolchester Beach Sunday and went on this thing." Postmarked 1911; $20

The little railroad at Tolchester Beach. Postmarked 1910; $25

LITTLE RAILROAD.   TOLCHESTER BEACH, MD.

General View of Amusements and Grounds, Tolchester Beach, Md.

General view of the
amusements and grounds.
Postmarked 1907; $12

The Wharf,
Tolchester
Beach,
Maryland.

The wharf at Tolchester
Beach. Circa 1905-07; $12

THE GREAT "LOUISE"   TOLCHESTER BEACH, MD.

VIEW OF TERRACE AND HOTEL.   TOLCHESTER BEACH, MD.

View of the terrace and hotel. Postmarked 1910; $12

The great *Louise* off
of Tolchester Beach.
Postmarked 1910; $12

TOLCHESTER HOTEL,   TOLCHESTER BEACH, MD.

The Tolchester Hotel.
Postmarked 1910; $12

The pier and steamers *Louise*, *Emma Giles*, and *Annapolis*. Postmarked 1909; $12

No. 157. The Susquehanna, Baltimore, Md.

The *Susquehanna* flying the Tolchester Company flag. Circa 1905-07; $10

Wharf at Tolchester Beach, Md.

The wharf and entrance arch. Circa 1907-12; $12

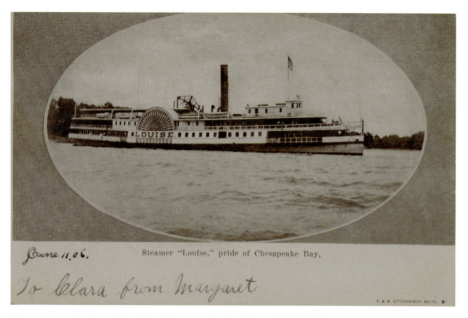

The steamer *Louise*, pride of the Chesapeake Bay. Dated 1906; $12

Steamer *Louise* with her decks overflowing with excursionists. Circa 1907-12; $8

A nighttime view of the steamer *Louise* on the Chesapeake Bay. Postmarked 1909; $8

Steamer *Louise*, Tolchester's popular excursion boat, entering berth at Light Street wharf, Baltimore. Circa 1907-12; $8

Steamer *Annapolis*, one of the boats of the Tolchester Beach Improvement Company. Circa 1907-12; $8

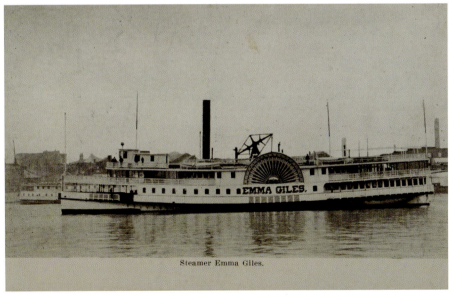

Steamer *Emma Giles*, popular boat of the Tolchester Beach Improvement Company. Circa 1907-12; $10

A souvenir from Tolchester Beach. Postmarked 1909; $8

The excursion steamer *Louise* returning to Baltimore from Tolchester Beach. Circa 1905-07; $10

Just arrived at Tolchester Beach. Circa 1905-07; $10

Familiar sights at Tolchester Beach. Circa 1905-07; $10

The small railroad at Tolchester Beach. Postmarked 1912; $15

The new Excursion House. Postmarked 1909; $8

Enjoying the beach. Postmarked 1911; $8

The steamer *Susquehanna*, one of the boats of the Tolchester Beach Improvement Company. Circa 1907-12; $12

Steamer *Louise* landing excursionists. Circa 1909-15; $8

The Hotel Tolchester. Circa 1907-15; $8

The new arch entrance.
Circa 1909-15; $8

The hotel at Tolchester Beach. Circa 1907-15; $8

Proper beach attire. The Chenoweth
Studio (photo) at Tolchester Beach.
Circa 1907-09; $12

All ready for a swim with beach bonnet and surf shoes. Circa 1907-09; $12

Children's beachwear. Circa 1907; $12

Men's beach attire. The Chenoweth Studio (photo) at Tolchester Beach. Circa 1907-09; $12

Photo taken by the Beach
Photo Studio at Tolchester
Beach. Circa 1907-09; $15

Fashionable ladies beachwear.
Circa 1907-09; $12

The new Excursion House.
Postmarked 1916; $8

The Switchback Railway at Tolchester Beach. Circa 1916-25; $10

The race track and horses. Circa 1916-25; $10

VIEW OF PICNIC GROUNDS, TOLCHESTER BEACH, MD.

View of the picnic grounds.
Circa 1920s; $10

THE GOAT TRACK, TOLCHESTER BEACH, MD.

The goat track was
popular with youngsters.
Circa 1920s; $10

View of the amusements. Circa 1916-25; $10

The steamer *Louise* on the way to Tolchester Beach. Circa 1916-25; $8

Bathing at Tolchester Beach. Postmarked 1921; $8

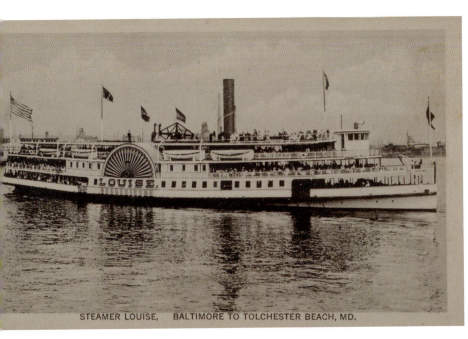

STEAMER LOUISE, BALTIMORE TO TOLCHESTER BEACH, MD.

Steamer *Louise* taking excursionists to Tolchester Beach. Circa 1920s; $8

STEAMER LOUISE, MOONLIGHT ON THE CHESAPEAKE.

Steamer *Louise* navigating the Chesapeake Bay on a romantic moonlit night. Circa 1916-25; $8

EXCURSIONISTS LUNCHEON AT TOLCHESTER BEACH MD

In the picnic grounds. Handwritten message on the backside reads: "We are having a nice time. We are now going across the Chesapeake Bay. The water is fine. Wish you were here." Postmarked 1916; $8

ENTRANCE TO PICNIC GROUNDS WITH EXCURSION HOUSE IN BACKGROUND.

TOLCHESTER BEACH, MD.

The entrance to the picnic grounds with the Excursion House in the background. Circa 1920s; $8

TOLCHESTER HOTEL ANNEX, TOLCHESTER BEACH, MD.

The Tolchester Hotel Annex. Circa 1920s; $8

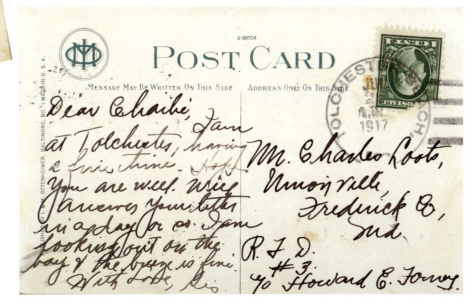

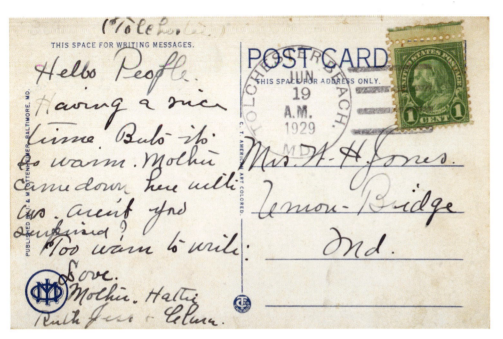

THIS SPACE FOR WRITING MESSAGES.

POST CARD

THIS SPACE FOR ADDRESS ONLY.

Hello People.
Having a nice
time. But it's
too warm. Mother
came down here with
ours. Aren't you
surprised?
Too warm to write.
Love.
Mother. Hattie
Ruth Jess + Helen.

Mrs. H. H. Jones.
Lemon Bridge
Md.

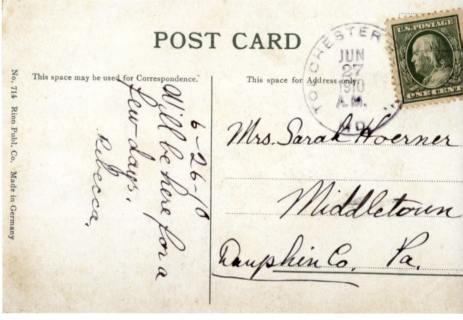

POST CARD

This space may be used for Correspondence.

This space for Address only.

6-26-10
Will be here for a
few days.
Rebecca.

Mrs. Sarah Hoerner
Middletown
Dauphin Co. Pa.

The Stars you meet here.

AT TOLCHESTER

The stars you meet at Tolchester.
Postmarked 1916; $7

Excursion House and Pier, Tolchester Beach, Md.

The Excursion House and pier.
Circa 1920s; $8

72 Excursionists Entering Tolchester Beach, Md.

Excursionists entering Tolchester Beach. Circa 1920s; $8

Whirl-Pool Dips, Tolchester Beach, Md.

WHIRL-POOL DIPS.

The Whirl-pool Dips Roller Coaster. Postmarked 1920; $12

Tolchester Beach and the steamer *Louise*. Circa 1916-25; $15

The Amusement Parlor at Tolchester Beach. Handwritten message on the backside reads: "Sure wish you were with us. Having a fine time. Just did make the boat." Postmarked 1932; $10

The Whirl-Pool Dips Roller Coaster. Circa 1920s; $12

Bathing Beach, Tolchester Beach, Md.

The bathing beach.
Circa 1920s; $10

South Side, Hotel Tolchester, Tolchester Beach, Md.

South side of Hotel Tolchester. Circa 1920s; $10

Picnic Grove, Tolchester Beach, Md.

The picnic grove. Circa 1920s; $10

Steamer Express, Baltimore, Md.

The steamer *Express*.
Circa 1925; $8

Steamers *Louise*, *Emma Giles*, and
Annapolis from the bathing beach.
Circa 1920s; $10

Steamers, Louise, Emma Giles and Annapolis, and Bathing Beach, Tolchester Beach, Md.

STEAMER TOLCHESTER

BALTIMORE'S LARGEST EXCURSION STEAMER

Steamer *Tolchester*, Baltimore's largest excursion steamer. Handwritten message on the backside reads:
"This is the new boat, we are all here." Postmarked 1933; $15

STEAMER TOLCHESTER, BALTIMORE'S LARGEST EXCURSION STEAMER ON THE WAY TO TOLCHESTER BEACH, MD.

Steamer *Tolchester* on the way to Tolchester Beach. Postmarked 1936; $7

TB-1—Bingo on Midway, Tolchester Beach, Md., on Chesapeake Bay

BINGO

5B-H1091

Bingo on the Midway.
Circa 1945-49; $8

TB-2—Pavilion and Hotel, Tolchester Beach, Md., on Chesapeake Bay

The Pavilion and hotel. Circa
1945-49; $8

5B-H1092

TB-3—Children's Playgrounds and Golf Course, Tolchester Beach, Md., on Chesapeake Bay

5B-H1093

Children's playgrounds and golf course. Circa 1945-49; $8

TB-4—"Bear Mountain" Boat at Pier, Tolchester Beach, Md., on Chesapeake Bay

5B-H1094

The *Bear Mountain* boat at the pier. Circa 1945-49; $8

TB-5—Miniature Railway and Pennyland, Tolchester Beach, Md., on Chesapeake Bay

5B-H1095

The miniature railway and Pennyland. Circa 1945-49; $8

The Dips and café. Circa 1945-49; $8

The bathing beach.
Circa 1945-49; $8

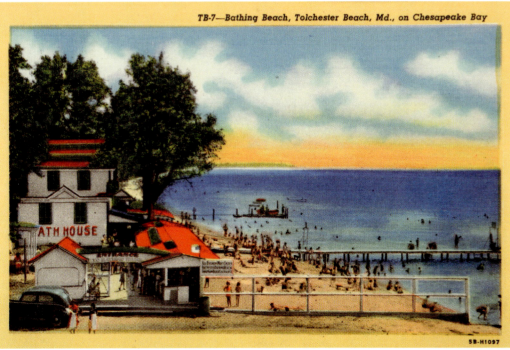

TB-8—Amusement Section, Tolchester Beach, Md., on Chesapeake Bay

THE WHIP

5B-H1098

The amusement section. Postmarked 1949; $8

TB-8—Steamer Tolchester, Baltimore, Md.

The steamer *Tolchester*. Circa 1948-49; $7

8B-H1487

TOLCHESTER BEACH, MARYLAND, ON CHESAPEAKE BAY

The bath house and bathing area. Circa 1950s; $15

TOLCHESTER BEACH, MARYLAND, ON CHESAPEAKE BAY

The Tolchester Hotel. Handwritten message on the backside reads: "Sure is hot here. The boat ride was swell, almost 2 hours on the water. The girls are going swimming." Postmarked 1957; $15

TOLCHESTER BEACH HOTEL, TOLCHESTER BEACH, MARYLAND,
ON CHESAPEAKE BAY

The Tolchester Beach Hotel and Excursion Pavilion. Circa 1950s; $15

S. S. TOLCHESTER, FROM BALTIMORE TO TOLCHESTER BEACH, MARYLAND, ON CHESAPEAKE BAY

The S. S. *Tolchester*, from Baltimore to Tolchester Beach. Circa 1950s; $15

A view from the end of the pier.
Circa 1950s; $8

Steamer *Bay Belle* unloading
excursionists. Circa 1950s; $8

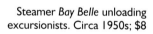

The *Bay Belle*; last excursion boat to stop at Tolchester Beach. Circa 1950s; $8

The amusement area. Circa 1950s; $8

Big New Steel Excursion Steamer

"TOLCHESTER"

Plying between Baltimore, Md. and Tolchester Beach — the Beautiful Excursion Resort — Fine Salt Water Bathing — Delicious Meals

Tolchester Co., Pier 16 Light St., Baltimore, Md.

S.S. TOLCHESTER, FROM BALTIMORE TO TOLCHESTER BEACH, MARYLAND, ON CHESAPEAKE BAY

AUTOMOBILE SQUARE, THE CHESAPEAKE HOTEL, BETTERTON, MD.

Greetings from
BETTERTON
MARYLAND

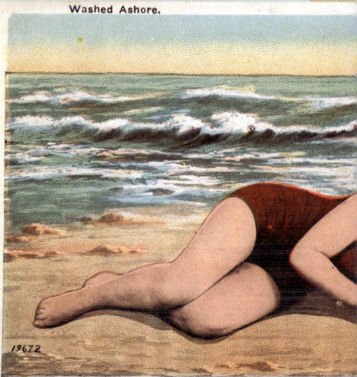

Washed Ashore.

19672